Transcending Bipolar Disorder

My Own True Story of Recovery from Mental Illness

B. Robert Jameson

iUniverse, Inc.
Bloomington

Transcending Bipolar Disorder
My Own True Story of Recovery from Mental Illness

Copyright © 2012 B. Robert Jameson

All rights reserved. No part of this book may be used or reproduced by any means, graphic, electronic, or mechanical, including photocopying, recording, taping or by any information storage retrieval system without the written permission of the publisher except in the case of brief quotations embodied in critical articles and reviews.

iUniverse books may be ordered through booksellers or by contacting:

iUniverse
1663 Liberty Drive
Bloomington, IN 47403
www.iuniverse.com
1-800-Authors (1-800-288-4677)

Because of the dynamic nature of the Internet, any Web addresses or links contained in this book may have changed since publication and may no longer be valid. The views expressed in this work are solely those of the author and do not necessarily reflect the views of the publisher, and the publisher hereby disclaims any responsibility for them.

Any people depicted in stock imagery provided by Thinkstock are models, and such images are being used for illustrative purposes only.

Certain stock imagery © Thinkstock.

ISBN: 978-1-4697-8480-9 (sc)
ISBN: 978-1-4697-8482-3 (hc)
ISBN: 978-1-4697-8481-6 (e)

Printed in the United States of America

iUniverse rev. date: 2/16/2012

This book is dedicated to the Glory of God, Who is the Source of all true healing, the Giver of knowledge, and the One who answers prayers.

For Linda, the love of my life;

for my children and for yours,

who show that life is worth fighting for.

Disclaimer

The information contained in this book describes my story and how I successfully recovered from bipolar disorder. I am not a medical doctor, nor am I a psychiatrist or a psychologist, and thus I am not authorized or qualified to give such medical advice. For any medical issues, it is critical to consult a qualified doctor. Such a role as I can play is limited to providing an example of a recovered individual, and giving examples of what strategies, attitudes and behaviours worked for me. I believe this role is valuable but must not replace the role of a doctor or psychologist.

Contents

Preface. xi
Acknowledgments. xiii
Introduction. xv

Part 1 My Story

Chapter 1: Lead-up and First Hospitalization—
  Breakdown 3
Chapter 2: Second Hospitalization and
  Aftermath—Picking up the Pieces 13
Chapter 3: Third Hospitalization—Power Overload . . 23
Chapter 4: Fourth Hospitalization—Confrontation
  and Standoff 35
Chapter 5: Fifth Hospitalization—Victory 49
Epilogue 59

Part 2 Transcending Bipolar Disorder

Foreword 63
Chapter 6: Newly Diagnosed with Bipolar Disorder . . 65
Chapter 7: Some Thoughts on Hypomania, Mania
  and Psychosis 67
Chapter 8: Dealing with and Overcoming Depression . 71
Chapter 9: Transcending Bipolar Disorder:
  Strategies and Exercises 77
Chapter 10: Advice for Those Trying to Help 87
Conclusion 91

Preface

Slowly, the fragments of sanity began to come back together. All four limbs were tied down to a hospital bed. I was isolated in a separate section of the emergency ward at the hospital. Everything was white in the room, so antiseptic by look and smell that it seemed nothing could take root and grow there, not even bacteria. A hostile set of fluorescent white lights beat down on me. At some point my clothing had been removed and I had been dressed in a hospital gown, but I didn't remember when.

I remembered other events, though.

I remembered the agony of the insanity. The shame of the things I had done.

Life no longer seemed familiar. How could I have acted that way? Said those things? *Done* those things? What had happened to me?

As my sanity returned, I had to face my new reality.

Bipolar disorder.

Acknowledgments

I would like to acknowledge everyone who helped and supported me throughout my illness. First and foremost, I would like to thank my dear wife, Linda, who stood by me throughout. I honestly don't think I would have made it without you. I would like to thank my parents for their support before, during and after my illness. Their presence was a big help too. I would like to thank my parents, my brother and sister, and my in-laws for being involved in my life. I owe a debt of gratitude to the company where I used to work for holding my job for me despite many work absences, and bearing with me until I was well. I would also like to thank my former coworkers (and still friends!) for their friendship.

I would like to thank the fellow members of my online spiritual forums for inspiration and some helpful feedback on this text. Most of all, I would like to thank God for healing me from bipolar disorder and giving me the inspiration to write this book.

Introduction

This book is a story of hope, of transcending darkness to arrive at a place of happiness. I wrote it for several reasons. The first reason is to give glory to God in gratitude for my healing. Aside from that I have written to describe how I was healed and to provide an example of someone who completely recovered from this illness. To put it frankly, I believe there is too much gloom and fatalism over this illness. If there are cases of cancer remission, why is it so impossible to believe in cases of bipolar recovery?

The first part of the book describes my struggle with the illness, from before my first episode in 2002 until the healing from the illness in 2006. I did not get better all at once—it was a progression toward healing that took several years.

There were two parts of the initial diagnosis that were most troubling. The first was that I'd had many experiences that were completely alien to me. I was shocked at my outrageous behaviour and was afraid of myself and what I might do next. This book describes a few of my "outrageous behaviours" without (I hope) descending into sensationalism. The readers who feel alienated as a result of bipolar disorder can rest assured that they are not alone, that others have shared in strange thoughts and behaviours.

The second part of the bipolar disorder diagnosis that greatly troubled me was that I was told I would have to take medication for the rest of my life. I had a negative attitude toward psychoactive medication, and frankly, I didn't want to take it. I didn't want the side effects that I felt sure medication would present. Furthermore, I felt taking this kind of medication was a crutch that was preventing me from healing. This attitude was responsible for several relapses, in retrospect. I would say now that medication does help stabilize a person, and while taking medication, he or she can work on their personality and spiritual development, analogous to high-wire performers who work with a net below them. If I can change anyone's mind to take or stay on his or her medication, this book will be worth it.

I believe I am completely cured of bipolar disorder and no longer need medication, yet as you will read, I am still taking a light dosage every day. My wife and doctor want me to maintain this dosage, and I am complying (which is a miracle in itself!) even though I feel it is not really medically necessary. There is nothing further for me to prove in this area. As of writing this book, it has now been more than five years since my last and final bipolar relapse and hospitalization. I am not experiencing any side effects with the medication I am taking.

The second part of the book was written as a guide to help those who want to overcome bipolar disorder, as well as for family and friends of bipolar sufferers who would like to know what they can do to help. During my recovery, there were many setbacks. I hope to shed light on what went wrong in my case so that the healing process may be shorter and smoother for someone who wants to follow my example and advice.

I hope you enjoy this story and can find information herein that may be of benefit to you or others. Happy reading!

Part 1
MY STORY

Chapter 1:

Lead-up and First Hospitalization—Breakdown

There's no limit to how high you can go.
—Ken (my boss).

It's hard to know where to start the story about the effects of bipolar disorder in my life. The roots were very deep. Problematic trends accelerated and started to blossom in 2001, and the illness bore its evil fruit in 2002. I would say 2001 was when I started to go off the rails in a serious way.

To give a bit of background: I married my wonderful, beautiful wife, Linda, in 1998. I finished my Ph.D. in 1999, and after another short stint working at a university for a year and a half, I began my career as a professional medicinal chemist at a pharmaceutical company in Montreal in January 2001.

I was excited about the job; it was my dream job, and I worked hard at it. Sometimes there was quite a bit of pressure, but it was a relief to meet the deadlines. Despite my hard work and the praise of my superiors, I felt that I was not very good at the job. This was a stress that began to mount as the successful year went by. I began to feel like I needed an edge. Along with this was the sense that I had professionally climbed to a plateau: I had earned the PhD I had been seeking for five years, and then I landed the job I had wanted for many years. So what now? I decided to try to become a director at the company, but it was a goal I wasn't as passionate about. I began to seek something else, something less tangible.

I had been wearing glasses since grade four. I became interested in recovering clear eyesight without the need of glasses, a claim being made by some doctors and alternative/New Age medical practitioners. During the course of reading about this, I learned of the claim that psychic powers could be augmented as well, and I hoped that this could help me perform better in my career. Seeking out psychic abilities for such a selfish purpose would lead me into trouble and destabilize my grip on reality.

I performed a series of eye exercises on a regular basis. One of them was to wear a patch over each eye in turn, for at least a half hour. When I used my left eye and covered my right, however, I found that I would get very tired and had difficulty in keeping my weaker left eye open. I learned that if I drew pictures while wearing the patch over my right eye this tiredness would not occur. The content of the pictures I would draw in this way, however, was gruesome and disturbing. I think it best not to describe the grotesque contents of these pictures, but they were a sign that something was wrong with my psyche. I was shocked to find that my mind had produced such pictures.

By the end of 2001 I had completed the first year of my pharmaceutical career. I felt unsuccessful and was afraid of the performance rating I would receive. I was becoming obsessed with improving my eyesight, which hadn't made much progress. I was having trouble sleeping some nights, worrying over minor problems or events at work.

I received a shock in February 2002. I received my rating for my performance of 2001—and it was outstanding. One might imagine that this would be a pleasant surprise, but it was not whatsoever to me. I was told by my boss, Ken, "There is no limit to how high you can go in this organization." This unsettled me greatly. I had an inferior view of myself relative to others in the company and felt I didn't fit in very well. Although I wrote earlier that I had set a goal for myself to be a director, part of me did not want it. I wasn't even sure I wanted to keep working in the industry. It also created added pressure for me to live up to a rating that I didn't feel I had earned and didn't have the ability to match. I was starting to crack.

So these were the first cracks in my sanity. Next came the hammer blow.

* * *

It was a cool Thursday evening in March. Linda and I were relaxing in the front room of our modest apartment, watching television. At about nine o'clock I received a phone call from my sister. She had some news that she wanted to tell me in private. I still remember how she told me.

"I have something to tell you. Uncle Calvin ... was not a nice man."

In my head, as soon as she told me that and before she went into detail, I frantically thought: *No, anything but this!* She told me he had sexually abused her while she was a child, thirty years ago, and she had only remembered it now, under hypnosis during therapy.

Then another thought came to me: perhaps he had sexually abused me as well. I asked, "Do a lot of pedophiles molest both boys and girls?" I thought she would know this since she was a psychologist.

"Most pedophiles"—she spat the word out with disgust—"choose only one sex."

We talked for a half hour. After I got off the phone, I told my wife my sister's news, and I wept. I wanted to be loyal to my sister and support her during this awful time. I also wasn't sure what my parents' reaction would be, and I wanted them to stand by her as well. I wanted them to believe her, but I was not sure they would.

I didn't sleep that night, and the next day at work was really difficult. I wondered whether people around me were sexual abusers or had been sexually abused as children. I was angry at the world around me.

Friday night we drove to visit Linda's family in Toronto. It was a welcome oasis of peace away from the insanity I was facing. Perhaps if I had received that call on a Sunday night and had to face a full work-week without respite, I might have been hospitalized right then. The news rocked me to the core, and I was barely able to function.

When we got back from Toronto, I talked to my parents. They were really worried about how my sister, my brother and I were all coping with this story. They said that at first they hadn't really believed the story, but my brother's reaction as well as mine convinced them that there was something to it. I was very angry at them. I didn't sense that they understood the gravity of what had been revealed; they didn't see it or didn't care about it. They decided to pay me a visit, as my brother had suggested they should. Linda, my parents and I decided to take a drive over to Toronto, and then after a visit with Linda's family, my parents would drive us back. It was Easter time.

I felt an intense hatred of Uncle Calvin that was poisoning my mind. I was terrified and furious that he had perhaps done something to me as well as angry that he had hurt my sister. I felt debased, ashamed and disgusted. While Linda and I were visiting with her family, I had a hallucination. At one point, she turned and looked at me, and instead of seeing her face, I saw his old face grinning at me, looking the way he had a few years before his death. I was shocked and discomfited. I realized I couldn't go on like this.

That night, I dreamt something I can't remember now, but the message was that anything he had done to me was in the past. I woke up and it was Easter Sunday, a good time to put the past behind and forgive him, or at least let it go.

As soon as I did, the anger I had been feeling just shifted onto my parents. How had they let this happen? Why were they carrying on in such a nonchalant way—how could they, after this had happened?

While still in Toronto, I spent some time walking with my

father. He said to me, "I feel like I should go and visit your sister. I feel like it will be hard for me, but I should go." I considered that very selfish of him to be thinking about how hard it would be for him to go instead of thinking how he could best help his daughter. Then he started talking about me, and he said, "I am not worried about you at all."

I wondered how he could be so blind and uncaring. Linda's father later noticed there was something wrong with me, and he tried to snap me out of it by talking to me about light subjects, but there was nothing he could do.

The next day my parents, Linda and I drove back to Montreal. I was quiet in the car.

"A penny for your thoughts," my mom said.

I decided to tell her what was on my mind. "I think Uncle Calvin might have done something to me too."

We talked for a while, and my mom, sister and I all cried. My dad was unsettled and said he had to take a break from driving. Eventually we got back to Montreal. My parents would stay the night. I decided to take a day off work and spend it with them before they went back home.

Before we went out to dinner, my dad was irritated with me. He kicked me in the leg and said, "I'll jab you in the solar plexus," and made a threatening gesture. I glared at him, furious.

Dinner was a cold, unfriendly meal. As it was ending, my parents said they would like to call my sister. They could see I was very angry, and they were conciliatory. "Do you have any advice on what I should say to her?" my father earnestly asked me.

I pretended to think for a moment. "No," I replied coldly.

Fortune cookies came. Mine said: you long for perfection. My mother's said: your luck is about to change. I don't remember the other ones.

Back at our apartment, it was time to call. My dad offered to visit my sister, but she said she didn't want him to come.

"Well, I have church," he said.

As soon as I heard that, I completely lost control. I began to scream and cry uncontrollably. My dear wife came over and put her arms around me, and tears ran down her face. My mother also came over. "Shhh," she said quietly, "the neighbours will hear."

I turned away from her and clung to Linda. I began to scream and cry even louder. I said to Dad, "Do I have to beg for your love?" and got down on my knees.

"For heaven's sake," he said, irritated and surprised.

My wife, my mother and I went into the office. I regained my composure after a minute or so. I had stopped crying and was calm. "I didn't know I had that in me," I said ruefully.

Despite this cathartic release of grief and hurt, something was still missing. I didn't feel as if my parents were really sorry enough about what had happened. They didn't seem very engaged in the whole situation. Something was wrong with the picture. I felt like the whole situation was a puzzle that I needed to piece together, but some of the pieces were missing. The whole night I stayed awake praying. I prayed for God's power, saying I didn't care if I died, but I needed to know the truth. I prayed and prayed.

The next morning was a sunny day, but the daylight seemed white and cold instead of a warm yellow. My wife was leaving for work. I told her I loved her. I didn't tell her I wasn't sure I would survive the day.

After she was gone, I went out to see my parents. I talked to them for about five minutes, but I don't remember everything I said. I remember saying that if Uncle Calvin had molested my sister, I would have burned him alive. I didn't really know what I was saying. Then I said to my dad to get down on his knees and beg for my forgiveness for spanking me when I was in grade two.

"But what about?" he began.

"Get on your knees," I screamed at him.

"Okay, son, for you I will." He got on his knees and said, "I beg for your forgiveness."

Then I got down on my knees in front of him and said, "I love you, Dad. I wasn't trying to be better than you."

Madness overtook me, and I went over to my mother and told her to beg for my forgiveness too. On my way over, an inner voice said to me, *Don't do this!* but I was too confused and power-mad to listen. I lived with the shame of that for years afterward. The only thing I can say to defend myself was that I was also trying to take the suffering away from my parents, not just get back at them.

After this transpired, my parents stayed around for a few hours and then left me and went home. When Linda came home that evening, my parents called and said I was sick and needed to see a doctor. I told my mother I never wanted to see her again, and that Uncle Calvin was my real father.

I didn't sleep that night either and made it only through the next day before I was hospitalized. I actually went to work the next morning, but everyone could see something was seriously wrong with me. My boss, Ken, told me to take the rest of the week off. I walked home and started acting even crazier, losing control of my actions, acting out with strange gestures, doing strange rituals. My wife was confused and frightened by my actions, and she called 911 on me, with good reason.

The police and ambulance personnel came and took me away. When I saw the ambulance I began to resist, but they easily overpowered me. My insanity progressed even further, and I looked into the eyes of the personnel and could feel their suffering. This was not an intellectual type of understanding. I experienced the fullness of their pain even more than *they* were consciously aware of it. It was terrible suffering, more than I could endure. I screamed out to God so that He would help me. A sudden feeling of transcendent peace came, confused as it was with the suffering of insanity.

While still in the ambulance an unbelievable thing happened. My life began to flash backward before my eyes. Everything was rewinding. I could feel pubic hair in my mouth and was trying to spit it out. The ambulance staff thought I was spitting at them and covered my mouth with a cloth. I kept spitting—the cloth became wet, and I could hardly breathe, although I was panting furiously.

I thought I was going to die of suffocation. I felt a new spirit being born into me, and although it was a stillbirth, it was okay.

Then I had a vision.

A father holds his son in his arms. The baby looks up at his father with love and gurgles with joy. The father coos gently to his son, expressing a love beyond words. They both have a light in their eyes that joins them together, and they are one in it.

There's a new story now, and it begins with that. Or is that the epilogue, or chapter 3?

I eventually lost consciousness in the ambulance. For a moment I started speaking in tongues, calling out for a guru. Then I blacked out.

At the hospital

I temporarily regained consciousness once admitted to the hospital. It would not be particularly illustrative to describe the insanity that initially transpired there. After maybe an hour and a half I came back down to earth. One poignant thing I remember was a lady saying to me, "Bon courage, monsieur." Was she an angel? After I came down, I slept for a full day.

I was admitted to a room on the psychiatric ward. The assigned psychiatrist came by to see me. She asked how I was, and I said I was tired. I asked her for a glass of water, but she said I should ask the nurses. How was that for effective delegation of labour? Whatever it was, it sure came across as cold.

When I was fully awake, I became scared that I would never be released from the hospital. I asked a nurse how long I would be held for, and she told me it was usually a matter of weeks before someone is released, not months or years. That was a great comfort to me. My attitude was to be completely compliant with the doctors and nurses so they would let me go as soon as possible.

That night there was a "code white." A code white is when a patient is resistant, perhaps violently so (as was the case this time), and needs to be restrained. The patient fought bravely but futilely, and he was restrained hand and foot in the pink room. The pink room was a room with only a bed equipped with restraints, an adjoining washroom, and a cute little peek-a-boo window that opened at the nurses' station so they could peek in at the patient whenever they wanted. I didn't know much about it this first hospitalization—I found out later. After the code white, all the patients were assembled so the staff could calm their fears about the event. Someone asked if the bed was fixed to the floor so it wouldn't rise off the ground. The orderly assured that it was fixed.

Back in my room, which I shared with three other men, one of my roommates said to me that he was happy to see me and that he'd been afraid it was me who had been put in the pink room.

Suddenly there was a knock at the door.

An older man, about fifty-five, with wild eyes was staring at me. "Robert, there is a meeting outside," he lisped.

"We already had the meeting," I replied.

"There is another one," he said.

"No, I am not going."

"I want to sleep with you. In your bed."

We were all shocked, and my roommates told him to go away. I was afraid, but my roommates said they would keep watch to make sure he wouldn't come back. They told me his name was Ben, and he was stone-cold crazy. It was a creepy experience. I had trouble sleeping again that night.

After the first few days, the time passed quickly. The medication I was taking was making me ravenous. I was eating two meals at dinnertime instead of one. I was rapidly gaining weight. Also, one of the medications was given under the tongue, and it was making my tongue swell so much that I sounded foolish when I spoke. I complained to the doctor about the side effects, but she wouldn't listen. Apart from that, the medication was affecting my mind, making me less creative, an asset I needed in my career.

This medication acted as though it was a brace inside my brain. What it felt like is somewhat difficult to explain. Whenever I would want to consider something "off to the side", meaning a sort of strange thought, it would be as though the brace would stop me, snapping my focus back to the front, with a sensation of "No, we are not going to think about that." That is what it felt like to me.

I asked my psychiatrist how long I would have to take my medication. She replied firmly that the antipsychotic would probably be needed for about a year, but the other medication I would have to take for the rest of my life. I was devastated by this news.

I tried writing down all the insane thoughts that were going through my mind during this time, and I wanted to give them to the doctor, but she wouldn't read them. She asked for a five second summary. All in all, she didn't have much time for me. I went along with everything because I just wanted to be released from the hospital.

Throughout my hospitalization, my wife and my parents, who had returned to Montreal, visited me every day and were a great comfort to me.

Finally, three weeks after I had been brought by ambulance to the hospital, I was released. It was great to be home with my wife again. I was, on the other hand, not the man I had been in 2001. I was still gaining weight at an alarming rate—between April and early June, I had gained twenty pounds. I was in denial that I had bipolar disorder; I thought it was just a temporary insanity that would soon pass, if it hadn't already. My medicine-induced speech impediment was a hindrance professionally as well, as was the effect on my creativity that I described earlier. All the more reason to completely ignore doctor's orders to take a month off from work, and to go right back to work three days after being released from the hospital!

Chapter 2:

Second Hospitalization and Aftermath—Picking up the Pieces

If you hurry, people will laugh at you.
    —Russian proverb

I resolved when I got back to work that the illness would not interfere with my career. I decided I would count my three weeks in the hospital as my three weeks of vacation for the year. Five weeks from when I was released from the hospital, I was set to go to a conference for Leading Young Canadian Organic Chemists in Victoria, BC. I was determined to go to this conference and make a great showing, followed by attending a five-day conference in Vancouver. My wife and the social worker who was seeing Linda and me following my release from the hospital both agreed it would be better not to attend the conference, but I had my heart set on it. My social worker insisted I was fragile, but I was in denial and would have none of it.

So a short time later I flew out to Victoria. I knew some of the professors who were attending the conference, and I met some new people as well. Altogether, there were about eight of us. The format for the presentations was a ninety-minute presentation on a whiteboard, which was freely interrupted by the rest of the attendees. Everyone was very eager and sharp, except me. Presenters started off their talks by drawing a map showing biographical information, including where they'd been born, where they'd been educated and which university they were currently affiliated with. After this introduction, they spoke on their research.

My turn came on the second day. I drew a map of southern Ontario and Quebec. "I was born in Cornwall, Ontario, and lived there for the first year and a half of my life" ... *(at which time I was sexually abused)*.... I began to stammer and lose control. I was having a panic attack right in front of everyone I wanted to impress. I was almost starting to cry. Professors could tell something was wrong with me, and some began to look at each other and smirk. I cut off the biography abruptly and started talking about my research, but I could no longer concentrate. I was more than fragile from the breakdown I'd had two months previously; I was still broken. I could barely control my writing on the whiteboard, and some professors were laughing at the distorted shapes I was drawing.

I fought my way through the talk, which must have been the worst I'd ever given. The whole thing only lasted about a half hour because there were hardly any questions during or after the presentation, since everyone was so shocked. After it was over, I had a quick lunch and went back to my room.

I went into the bathroom, to the place where I kept my pills. *So this is the best you can offer me?* I silently asked them. They didn't help at all with my courage, they made me fat, and they made me sound like an idiot with a fat tongue when I spoke. They made me feel less intelligent. *What kind of life is that?* I said to myself. I decided I would rather be dead than live like this, and I flushed all the pills down the toilet. Relieved and resolute, I rejoined the group of professors.

The last day of the conference passed uneventfully. After this we took a ferry to Vancouver for the second conference. I was fired up for it. I had my confidence back and a new lease on life. I wasn't bipolar anymore, I was off drugs and I wasn't taking any crap from life or anyone. Furthermore, if anyone had given me any crap before, I would pay them back for it now. I spent the week being somewhat obnoxious, but it was a fun time. I took the time to buy Linda a map of the world. I was going to tell her I could offer her the world if she would stay with me even though I had stopped my medication. She phoned me midway through the week and asked if I was still taking it. I lied and told her I was. I had decided to tell her the truth when I got back to Montreal. As the week passed I alternated between sleepless nights and nights of prolonged restful slumber, and on one of the nights when I couldn't sleep, I started acting out these strange Ninja gestures I had read once in a book some fifteen years before.

I flew back to Montreal on June 6, our wedding anniversary. My sanity was really starting to crack up on the plane. I started writing a patent for inducing spiritual states by administering large doses of antipsychotic drugs and then abruptly cutting them off (I suppose I shouldn't disclose that here, since it will become part of the prior art, making the idea no longer patentable). I was trying to manipulate people with my mind (and having some success, I might add). Life was getting creepier and creepier, but I made it to Trudeau Airport in Montreal. Much to my vehement irritation, no one was there to greet me.

A lady came up to me. "Monsieur, la joie?" she asked. *Where is your joy?* Was this another angel?

"Non, je ne ressens pas la joie," I replied obstinately. *I am not feeling joy.* She gave up and went away.

I phoned my wife and spoke angrily to her. She agreed eventually to come and get me, even though I could have easily taken a cab. After the call, I went over to the lady who had asked me about joy and told her I was happy now. She didn't seem to care. I had missed my last chance to come down from hypomania and was about to pay the price.

Linda came to get me, but she wasn't that pleased to see me. I told her I'd stopped my medication, and she was dismayed and shocked. I told her I wanted to go to the Holiday Inn, and she agreed. We got into a cab.

Linda asked the taxi driver to take us to the Holiday Inn. She was worried and agitated. I said nothing. The taxi driver could tell she was upset and wanted to have some fun at her expense. He laughed and said, "Which one? There are a lot of them."

"The Airport Holiday Inn," she replied.

He smirked and said he didn't know which one she meant. Seeing him tease my wife made me angry. I decided to scare him. I leaned forward, and glaring at him made a medium-pitched growl. Immediately he turned around in his seat and started driving. Linda was alarmed and told me to sit back and relax. Pleased with myself, I chortled for several blocks.

We checked into the Holiday Inn. Linda went out for a moment, as she said she was going to order some room service. A few minutes later there was a knock at the door. Guess who it was? Yes, of course. Linda had called 911 on me, and it was time for another trip to the hospital. I was furious and dropped my wedding ring on the floor. I was ready to fight with the police and paramedics, but they got me to calm down and comply after several minutes of reasoning. They also got me to pick up my wedding ring and put it on the night table in the hotel room. On my way to the ambulance I passed Linda. She was crying and said she would keep the ring for me. I felt angry and betrayed and didn't reply.

At the Hospital

I spent the night in the emergency room. There was nothing to eat, and I had not eaten since morning. A nurse had brought in cookies for her fellow staff, and I asked for one, but she wouldn't give me any. I could see the cookies through the window into the nurses' station from my bed, but I couldn't get them. Eventually the long, sleepless night passed, and morning came.

Next morning, Linda came to see me and was not pleased. She told me off, and she said she could tell I had lied to her about my medication over the phone when I was in Vancouver because I sounded "too good." We had a meeting with a psychiatrist, who, within about five minutes, assessed me as needing to be in the hospital. I was incensed. My attitude at being in the hospital was completely different this time. I was not compliant in any way, and I refused to take medication. Furthermore, the doctor who assessed me said my sense of humour was buried deep. I was going to show him!

Who should I run into when I was admitted? None other than Ben, the patient I had met during the first hospitalization. He came by my room and said, "Wait, I will tell you your name." He thought for a minute. "You are Robert, who tells the truth."

I smiled at him. I was feeling dangerous. "This time you tell only lies, cheeky monkey!" Challenging him this way, I held out my hand. He accepted the challenge, shook my hand and entered my room.

"Why are there so many chickens and only one rooster?" he asked.

I thought for a moment. "Because the rooster likes to screw," I said, punctuating the word *screw*. Then I began to yell, louder and louder, "Screw! Screw! *Screw!*"

Hospital staff came running. Hurriedly, they escorted Ben out of the room. "It sounded like you were having a karate fight," a nurse said to me.

On my second day of hospitalization I was given a routine blood test, and I took off the bandage they'd given me and put it outside on the wall. To me, it was like a Passover gesture, except rather than sacrificial animal blood to ward off death, I used my own.

One of my fellow inmates came to my room. He dared me about something; I can't remember what it was. The terms were that I would do anything he wanted. He looked at me and said, "Anything?" I laughed and said, "Anything."

I pointed at the wall inside my room. "But first I want you to see something. It is right here."

"Where?" he asked, looking where I pointed. There was nothing there but the bare wall.

"No, look outside. Right there."

He had to go outside to look, and then he couldn't come back in again. It worked. He walked away angrily. I had beaten him too.

After this fun escapade I looked down the hall. Someone was lying in bed. I closed their door all the way (which was not allowed) and then went to tell on them to the nurses. My little plan didn't get that far, however. About ten nurses and orderlies came to get me and put me in the pink room. I had been upsetting the other patients too much. The pink room was on the opposite side of the circular psychiatric ward.

"Wait, which way?" I shouted with urgency.

Quickly, everyone pointed. Some people pointed straight through the central wall of the ward, some people pointed around the circle clockwise, and others pointed around the circle counter-clockwise. I burst out laughing. They were all confused about their directions. That was my final trick for the day. They strapped me down, medicated me and I went to sleep.

Being tied down and forced to take medication broke my spirits somewhat, and I was no longer rebellious and feisty when I woke up again. My medication had been changed. The new medication was oral tablets, and I tolerated it much better. I no longer had such a huge appetite, and my tongue was no longer swollen. I found, however, that I was much more tired and lacked energy. I believed I was overmedicated, but the doctor didn't really listen to my complaints. I was kept in the hospital for three weeks and then released.

The Low Energy of Depression

I was off work for the next month. Far from rested, however, I felt exhausted every day, just from lazing around the house and sleeping. I felt I had no chance of ever becoming a director at my company now that I had shown such weakness. I was disheartened and had no goal beyond survival, but eventually my sick leave ran out, and I had to go back to work.

Fulfilling my duties at work on the dosage of medication I was taking was exhausting to the point of being beyond my ability.

I tried to fight the tired feeling, but I could not. One morning I came in and started work at nine o'clock. I put in my best effort and worked until exhaustion set in. Thinking it was about time to go home, I went back to my office and sat down. I looked at the clock. It read 9:50 a.m.

I started to use up my vacation time (I went back on the idea of counting my first hospitalization as a vacation), so that I had one week of work followed by one week of vacation. Alternating this way, I could barely make it through the summer. Eventually my vacation time was used up, and I had to face work without any more vacations. It was a pace I couldn't keep up, and I knew it. People at work could see I was not bearing up well.

One morning, I went to see my boss, Ken, and told him I couldn't take it anymore. "I know, you're not the same Robert since you've been sick," he said sadly with compassion. The drive that had sustained me for many years was gone.

I made an emergency appointment to see my psychiatrist. She told me I was depressed and needed to take at least two months off work. I went home and phoned this news to Ken. "Talk to the director," he said firmly.

I mistook his tone for lack of empathy. "I have a doctor's note!" I exclaimed.

"Everything is going to be okay. Don't worry, just call the director."

I did as Ken advised. The director was empathetic as well and said he was glad I'd called him. He said to take the time I needed and asked how long that would be.

"At least two months."

"Okay. If I know it will be that long, I can make arrangements for the project."

After the call, I was relieved. I called Ken back and thanked him for his advice. He said he could tell I had been depressed for a while and also knew I had been scared to lose my job. Now was the time to concentrate on getting well … or just curling up in an apathetic ball and not caring what happened next. The date was September 11, 2002.

I looked into finding a psychologist to help me feel better. I had recommendations for five different ones from my social worker. I phoned up the first one, but he sounded about as disheartened as I was, so I didn't choose him. I phoned the second one and talked to him. I told him I had been diagnosed with bipolar disorder. He immediately affirmed that this was a condition that required medication. For his candour, he lost me as a client right there.

Then I phoned the third name on the list: Anthony Sailes. He told me he was able to get results with clients in rapid fashion, and that I possibly wouldn't need to take medication in the future. He told me exactly what I wanted to hear. He charged a lot of money, in my opinion, but if he could do what he said, I would gladly pay.

I had my first appointment with Anthony later that week. While waiting in his outer office, there was strange music playing. I wondered how I had come to this and began to shake and almost cry. I realized it had been a long time since I had laughed, and I had come to believe that it would be betraying my sister and her pain if I had fun and laughed—not mean humour at others' expense like I had played in the hospital, but the kind of fun that people can laugh about together and feel good.

I had sessions with Anthony once a week, but my condition did not measurably improve for a while. I was also seeing my psychiatrist once a week. I had had a habit of asking my doctor repeatedly if she would lower my dosage of medication, which she typically refused. At some point during these months I became too apathetic to care about asking. She decided to put me on a low dose of antidepressant, risking the potential of mania that such medications can cause to bipolar patients. I was not pleased with this and didn't want another drug added to what I was already taking. She also lowered the dose of my antipsychotic medication. I made a decision—I would not take the antidepressant she prescribed. This decision, combined with the lowered dose of antipsychotic, made me feel much better. I was getting some control over my life again, and I was pulling out of the depression. I had much more energy than I did at my low point.

During this time, Linda and I decided to buy our first home. This decision convinced my psychologist that I didn't need much more help beyond follow-up on an infrequent basis. True to my word I returned to work two months after I had left, on November 11.

At the end of 2002 I had survived my first manic episode (or two if you count the late-May event as a separate one), and my first depression. I felt fairly good, and I was able to do my job well again, but none of the issues that had surfaced had really been resolved. I was functioning, but I was still wounded. I still wanted to be cured of bipolar disorder and medication-free. I was not finished with it, and it was not finished with me.

Chapter 3:

Third Hospitalization—Power Overload

Gorbatovo mogila ispravit.
—Russian proverb

It was January 2003. I had an evening appointment with Anthony. I told him I was feeling trapped and frustrated with my life, and how I wished I didn't have to take any medication.

"How is your rage?" he asked me. I don't know why he asked me that question, in that way, but he was right to ask.

"I feel very angry. I feel like I want to bite something. Just tear into it, you know?"

"I'm not really qualified to deal with some of the issues you're facing. I'm going to refer you to an energy therapist for energy balancing. There are a lot of quacks out there, but she can really do the things she says she can."

I wasn't sure what to think about this, but I agreed to it. I made an appointment with Susan, and next thing I knew, I was in her waiting area, which she shared with an acupuncturist. As I waited, I took in the surroundings. The floor was carpeted, which made the room feel quite homey. There were a few books in the corner, a statue of the Buddha, and a bare table in the centre of the room. Clients were obliged to take off their shoes outside the waiting area before they entered. Susan did her work in an office adjoining the waiting area.

"Hello," Susan said. "And what did Anthony send you here for?"

"He sent me here for energy measurements," I replied. I wasn't too hip to this New Age terminology and got it wrong. Anyway, it didn't matter. She seemed to know what I needed.

Susan assessed me using her technique and found that I was basically "a big train wreck" (my words, not hers). She said my first, second, fourth and seventh chakras were all not functioning. Chakras are energy centres localized at different places in the body, in a line from the base of the spine to the top of the head.

"You probably won't feel much happening for the first few sessions," she told me. She was wrong, however. As she worked on me, I could feel something happening right away. The first session had a small effect, as she measured it. After several more sessions, I felt quite different, a lot better, and my wife also noticed that the colour in my face was better. Susan also told me I was deficient in zinc and should take it in a large dose, such as was found in pumpkin seeds.

One day at home during this treatment period, I remember I was going up the stairs when a thought came to me: *All things work to good for those who serve the Lord.* The thought made me feel very good. At my next session, Susan said that my seventh chakra had balanced itself. This shows the importance of faith and love of God. I wouldn't say I did it myself, though; it was more a spiritual gift that was given to me.

After six sessions we were finished. She also said she had cleaned or cleared my cords that related to Uncle Calvin. I don't know what that means to this day. She was guilty of making elliptical statements sometimes. I was sad that the sessions were over because it had been an enjoyable experience having energy therapy with Susan. We had become friends—at least I thought of her as my friend—and I missed her.

Throughout 2003, life and work progressed in a favourable manner. Things were good at home, and the project I was working on at my job was highly successful. I had been exposed to alternative medicine, however, and had seen its power and the superior way it could help treat my psychological problems.

I could never look at the world the same way again. I began reading New Age literature and doing yoga. I didn't really work on my attitudes and behaviours to try to become a better person, though, which all the yoga and energy therapy in the world can't make up for, if these things are deficient. My psychiatrist slowly reduced my dosage of medication. Around this time, I decided to forgive Uncle Calvin for whatever he had done to my sister, and if anything, to me as well. It was a great relief.

Linda and I started trying for a baby. She had a miscarriage, a blighted ovum, which hit her really hard. It hit me too, but it hit her much harder. The miscarriage happened at the three-month mark, which is the time considered safe to tell others outside the family. I actually brought doughnuts to work to celebrate and then had to correct the story a week later. After a few months we tried again and she had another miscarriage. Following that, she successfully became pregnant.

One night, I was dreaming. It was just a typical senseless dream. Suddenly, a thought came to me: *I can choose other than this*. I held on to the thought, grinding it through my brain. Part of my mind became terrified, and I woke. Still, I held on to the thought. *I can choose other than this.* It felt like it was the end of my earthly life.

With lightning speed, some questions came: What about your parents? Can you forgive them? I answered silently that I forgave them. The thought came from a different angle: What about your sister? Can you forgive her? (The thought did not elaborate on what I had to forgive her for.) I answered that I forgave her. I was feeling an intense bliss, beyond description. Again it tried: What if your wife wakes up and finds you gone? I realized she would wake up with a corpse beside her and would have a lot of grief for an indeterminately long period. Instantly, I came back to myself. It's hard to explain, but it felt like I had been outside my body, on my right, had "inverted" somehow, and now I was back.

Another night around this time my wife and I were both sleeping. Acting unconsciously, I moved up against her, and when

I woke I felt a flow of energy between us. She resisted me, pushing back. Then the energy flow stopped. She didn't wake up, and I went back to sleep. I'd been a conduit for some form of energy flow to her, but I don't know what it accomplished. She didn't remember it; at least she never spoke of it to me, nor I to her.

Late that spring, my sister had a mental breakdown. She was put on medication, and as a result, no longer had any memories of Uncle Calvin sexually abusing her. She was no longer so sure it had happened. This development will have an important bearing on the story in chapter 4. Her psychiatrist told her that there are such things as false memories. These false memories seem real even though they never happened.

While Linda was pregnant, I am ashamed to say I didn't spend as much time with her as I should have. I let her go to sleep by herself most nights while I stayed up watching TV, reading or doing yoga. During this period of my life, winter 2003 and spring 2004, I found I didn't need that much sleep, usually six to eight hours on alternating nights.

As summer wore on, it was time for Linda to have our baby. She went into labour on September 3, and after almost a full day, Beatrice was born. She was a beautiful baby girl, and I was so proud. I had been off all medication for about four months at this time, and it helped me to stay up with Beatrice without being too tired the next day.

My wife and I did not settle easily into parenthood, however. I felt a considerable amount of strain and began to have trouble eating and sleeping. My parents came for a visit to help with the baby. I hadn't really wanted them there, but my wife insisted. I became really resentful of them again.

One evening at dinner, my mother said I didn't have any faith. I really resented that. I tried to just stuff the hurt down, but I couldn't. Before bed, I went to my mother and told her I wanted her to apologize for saying that. She denied she had said any such thing and then turned the tables on me and said she begged me to take my medication (she had found out several days before that I wasn't taking medication, but I hadn't been taking any for almost half a year by then).

All through the night I couldn't sleep. I was cracking again; I could feel it. I told my parents I was tired and was going to take a sick day. They told me I shouldn't miss work. I was feeling really sad and hopeless. I put on some music, a CD by Kitaro, to help me deal with the emotional pain. The first song was called "The Silk Road." It was a slow, beautiful song, and it helped me feel the sadness I had inside. I felt grief welling up inside, and I began to cry. My parents had gone upstairs.

The music continued after the song was over, and the next song was much different. It had a pounding rhythm and electric guitars. I felt a power surge from inside of myself. Fury welled up inside of me. I spoke from my soul to God. "*Gorbatovo mogila ispravit,*" I said. This is a Russian proverb. The translation is "Hunchbacks are straightened out by the grave." I had heard two meanings of the proverb. The first was that we should not make fun of others or look down upon them because everyone ends up the same way in the end. Later someone told me it refers to someone who is so crooked that only death can straighten him. When I said it, it was my prayer that I didn't know who was in the wrong, myself or my parents, but God, You must straighten them or me out because I am not willing to put up with this any longer.

As soon as I said this, I lost control. I pounded my fists on our family room table, so hard that it made both my hands bleed, and the table jumped off the floor. I was having a power overload. I was lying on the floor thrashing around, silently asking my father to help me up. No one helped me get up.

My mother came downstairs and said, "You scared the devil out of us!"

"That would be a good thing," I replied.

"Is this part of your meditation?" she asked.

"Yes," I answered.

My mother went away again. I had the sense of being unwanted as a foetus and felt the pain of this knowledge. As the music continued, I had a vision of history stretching out in a predictable, deterministic fashion, and then the crucifixion of Jesus Christ changing the trajectory of history. As the song ended, I got to my feet on my own, proud of myself and what I had accomplished, and took a bow.

I went out into the garage. It was dark. Again I started thrashing around on the floor. The cement floor was cold. I got to my feet and then went down on one knee, covering my eyes with my left forearm. The ring finger of my right hand went down, where, in the dark, it perfectly found a crevice.

At the same time a silent message came to me: *Go help Tom.* Tom was a patient I had seen in the hospital psych ward a week or so before. He had also been in the hospital when I was there in 2002, and I had been unfriendly toward him. Now I was given instructions.

I went back into the house after a few minutes. I felt completely relaxed, more so than I had ever felt in my life. All tension and stiffness had gone from my body. I had never felt so supple. The Kitaro CD had ended, and a relaxing CD was playing now. I felt ready to go to sleep. I heard the front door close, and I went to the door and locked it. "That should keep them out," I said to myself.

Next thing I knew, there were paramedics and a policeman in the family room. They told me to get dressed and come with them to the hospital. I refused and told them I was enlightened. They insisted. Again I refused. I thought they were bluffing, and they couldn't really take me out of my own home when I was calm and quiet. I told them the only way they would get me out of my house was if they carried me.

So carry me they did. On the way out of the house I passed my father and told him to take care of Beatrice. They took me out on a stretcher and drove me to the hospital. My father followed behind in his car. He was with me when we arrived at the hospital.

The paramedics were testing my blood pressure, as well as my pulse with a device applied to one finger.

"Do you believe in miracles, Dad?" I asked.

"Depends if they're good or not," replied my dad, somewhat huffily.

"Is there any other kind?" I asked rhetorically.

"I never thought about it before," he said, somewhat taken aback.

"Consider it now," I retorted. As I said the word "now" I flipped the pulse reader off of my finger, which happened just when the paramedics were finished measuring it.

My dad stayed with me in the emergency room for a few minutes, and then he left. There must have been a psychiatric assessment, but I can't remember it. The outcome of it wasn't in any doubt, anyway. It was time for another stay at the hospital.

In the Hospital Once Again

I insisted on being called Brett following admission to the hospital. Brett is my real first name, but I had never used it. Since birth, my parents called me Robert. Brett is also my father's first name. I introduced myself to fellow patients as Brett, and the nursing staff also agreed to call me Brett, even though they knew me from the past two hospitalizations as Robert. In keeping with my spiritual greatness, I needed a more spiritual name than Robert, I decided. I also refused to take any medication.

That evening I was lying down in my room when I heard someone yelling and cursing angrily. I recognized the voice as Tom's. I decided it was time to help him, as I had been instructed by the silent message.

I went out into the common room. Tom was sitting at a table with a young man whom I learned later was named Steve. Tom was agitated.

I pulled up a chair and joined them. "Hi, guys," I said. "My name is Brett."

I held out my hand to Tom. He wasn't paying much attention,

but he took my hand to shake. I squeezed his hand really hard, but only for a moment. From my work as a chemist, working with my hands each day, I had pretty strong hands. He looked at me, and I could see the paranoia and the burning mania in his eyes. Then I let go of his hand and smiled gently at him.

"Squeeze my hand," he said to me. I took his hand in both of mine and squeezed gently. Then I kissed his hand. I felt somewhat repulsed by the gesture, but I wanted him to know I would be his friend.

"You guys are fags," Steve said with disdain.

Neither of us paid any attention.

"I'm going now," I said to Tom. "Goodnight."

"Thanks for coming to see if I was all right," he replied. He had calmed down.

Before bedtime that night, I needed to brush my teeth. I had been brought into the hospital with nothing, so I had no toothbrush and no toothpaste. I went to Tom and asked him if I could borrow some toothpaste to put on my finger and brush my teeth with. He went over to the nurses' station to ask but suddenly changed his mind and walked away, saying nothing.

"Tom?" I called after him. But he didn't turn around.

That night, I didn't sleep. I spent some time talking to my roommate, Francois Leonard. He was a nice, gentle, older man, maybe sixty-five or seventy. I couldn't tell why he was in the hospital—he seemed quite normal to me.

The next morning I was upset that I couldn't see my daughter. I went to call home, but Tom was on the phone. I was too impatient to wait. I crowded up close to him and stared him down. "I need to use the phone," I said, not loudly but very firmly.

He stood his ground. "No!" he exclaimed. He held his forearm up against my throat so I could not press forward without choking myself. He knew some martial arts, apparently, and he looked a lot stronger than me, but I was not intimidated.

The altercation did not progress any further. Nurses came and separated us. I went back to my room. After a few minutes

I realized I had been in the wrong. It was breakfast time, and following that, I decided I needed to apologize. I didn't know where Tom's room was, so I asked Steve about it. He led me to the right place, where Tom was lying on his bed listening to music. He had earphones on, but the music was coming through so loud I could hear it well.

"I'm sorry about earlier this morning," I began.

"It's all right! Get Out!" he yelled in a tone that made it sound like it was anything but all right.

Steve and I left immediately. "Well, that went well, all in all," I said to Steve with relief.

Later on in the day I was able to phone my parents and convince them to bring Beatrice over so I could at least see her through the window. It was a great consolation to me, and I felt better afterward, although I missed her a lot.

That day and the next I spent time talking to other patients in the hospital. One patient had been teasing Tom. The man was an expert at tai chi. This was not just a manic, wild claim. I had seen him practice, and he really was highly skilled. He was tall and strong. I was in his room talking to him the day after the altercation with Tom, and he told me he was able to control people's minds. He went further to say he was about to do it now.

"I don't want any part of this!" I exclaimed. I left his room, but he came out after me.

Meanwhile, there was a disturbance out in the hall. Just down the hall, a nurse said to Tom, "I can't believe this," and went back to the nurse's station.

I went up to Tom. There was a smell of smoke coming from his room. Smoking in the hospital was strictly forbidden, and the patients in the psychiatric ward were not even allowed to keep their own cigarettes. I went up close to him and sniffed. He blew a whole breath-full of smoke right in my face. What did I do? I inhaled it. I breathed the evil spirit out of him. When he had no more breath, I coughed a little. He was speechless. Then I went over to the tai-chi man, held him by the wrist and brought him over to the nurses. "I accuse this guy of stirring up trouble." They didn't pay any attention, so I let the matter drop.

Tom had gone to sit on a chair in the common area. I went over to him and knelt on one knee so we were eye-to-eye.

The nurse who had caught him smoking came by and said, "What am I going to do with you, Tommy?"

"What is she going to do without you, Tommy? That is the best I can do, the rest is up to you." I had fulfilled my mission the best way I knew and wasn't going to try any more. I went to my room and rested.

Lunch was served about an hour later. I came to get my tray and looked for somewhere to sit. Tom looked at me. I really wanted to sit with him, but I resisted the urge. I looked away somewhat sadly and searched for somewhere else to sit.

"Here, sit here!" Tom called, motioning to a seat beside him.

I smiled and went to sit beside him. We ate without speaking. When I was finished, I said, "I love this guy." He was not really paying attention. "Up to a Point!" I punctuated the word "point" by slapping him in the face!

"Hey!" he said, but without anger.

I looked at him and smiled, showing him that I loved him and was glad I could help him.

"Here, sit here," he said. He motioned for me to sit in his seat, and he went off to his room. He was released from the hospital later that day, and I haven't seen him since. I hope he is well.

I don't know how much longer I lasted before the breakdown. The psychiatrist assigned to me wouldn't let me go outside because she considered me a "flight risk." That was an exaggeration, since I hadn't acquired levitation as one of my spiritual powers, as she should have known. A bit of fresh air might have kept me from crashing. Then again, maybe it wouldn't have. I was resentful of being kept against my will and was not sleeping at night.

I was lying on my bed one afternoon when Francois Leonard

came in. "I'm sorry I can't remember your name. I've been having electric shock treatments, and they've wiped out my memory."

"It's okay." I went over and gave him a hug. His sadness made me sad too, and I cried. I thought it inhumane that they were shocking the poor old man.

His nurse was giving him some information later, when I interrupted them.

"Treat this man with respect," I said to the nurse in an outraged tone.

Francois turned on me. "What right do you have to say these things?"

I was so angry I was speechless. Here I was trying to help the old coot, and that was how he treated me?

I was very agitated that night. In my mind I was preparing for battle. I felt like a warrior, and I was unafraid and ready to fight. My nurse must have had a suspicion something was going to happen because she wanted to give me medication by force, but there were no grounds, so she couldn't do anything.

The next thing I knew, it was morning. I was not in my bed, I was next to Francois's bed, and I had my left hand pressing on his throat, with my right hand stretching out parallel to the ground, out to my side. I was bellowing at the top of my lungs.

Francois woke up, terrified. "Nurse!" he cried out. Then he put both hands on my wrist to pull it off. Slowly, with both of his hands, he was able to push back somewhat. At that point, I put my right hand on his throat as well, and that was when all the nursing staff came in. They immediately took me away to the pink room, tied me down and medicated me.

Instead of going to sleep, I became more and more excited. I began singing. Some of the patients, including tai-chi man came by and laughed at me. The hospital staff came and administered another tranquilizer, this time one that was supposed to last for two weeks. Even these "elephant tranquilizers" didn't knock me out. I kept singing. A social worker stopped in and told me to be quiet. I told her to look down on me from above if she wanted to command me. I don't think she understood what I meant.

The rest of this hospitalization ended with little fanfare. The psychiatrist doped me up with a heavy dose of medication, so much that I was stiff from it. I felt there was nothing to accomplish from not taking medication so I complied. I was also extremely frightened by my out-of-control and violent behaviour toward Francois Leonard and wanted the medication to curb such potential. If I hadn't complied, I would have been given the medication by force anyway. One good thing was that the medication I'd been given in 2002 was not added to my current meds. I begged the doctor not to prescribe that when she brought it up as a possible alternative, and she complied.

About three weeks after my admission, I was released and allowed to return home. I was more confused about myself than ever before.

Chapter 4:
Fourth Hospitalization—Confrontation and Standoff

> *The righteous will see the evil Inclination as a high mountain and wonder how we could have conquered such a high and huge mountain. The wicked will see the evil Inclination as a thread that is as thin as a hair. They will marvel and ask, "How could we not have overcome such a tiny thread of hair?"*
>
> —Philip S. Berg
> *The Essential Zohar: The Source of Kabbalistic Wisdom*

After I was released from the hospital, I made appointments with Anthony and Susan, my former helpers. The first meeting was with Anthony. I hadn't seen him in more than a year, and he had changed his office around, reversing the position of the therapist and the patient's chairs.

"Which chair should I sit in?" I asked grandiosely, implying I was now the expert.

He smiled and defused the situation. "Why don't you sit in this one?" he replied, motioning to the client's chair.

I described the events leading up to my hospitalization. "You never told me you spoke Russian," he said with surprise and some admiration, as I told him of the prayer I had made.

"There was a Russian postdoctoral fellow in my old lab," I explained. "He taught us some interesting expressions and proverbs like that one, and *'Pass be sheesh, lugay nas besheesh,'* which means 'If you hurry, people will laugh at you.'"

"This type of experience wouldn't happen to me because I am too grounded," Anthony said in a somewhat haughty but also somewhat jealous tone, as I described the out-of-control spiritual experience I'd had the morning I was hospitalized.

I described a feeling I had of being unwanted as a foetus, that I had connected with. When I described it, his face contorted for a moment, but he quickly hid it and regained professional composure. "Yes, it is possible to retain sensations that we receive at a very early age, even before birth," he said. He suddenly became irritated. "You should consider yourself lucky to have me as a therapist."

"And you should consider yourself lucky to have me as a client," I retorted.

He smiled. "I do. Well, if you want to know what I think, I think you had a Kundalini surge."

I had actually read a little bit about Kundalini energy. What I knew about it was that it is the energy that flows up the spine from its base during spiritual awakenings. I felt glamorous that such an awakening process had happened to me. It was flattering to my spiritual ego.

A few days after my appointment with Anthony, I had my appointment with Susan. She also had me describe the events that had taken place. When I told her that I had described myself as enlightened following the out-of-control experience, she said, "Wow!" She checked my energy and found that I would only need two sessions. I was disappointed to find I needed work.

"It would have been a miracle if you hadn't needed any work. Two sessions after a psychotic break is unheard of. What are your thoughts?"

"Anthony said I'd had a Kundalini surge." This sounded much more glamorous than a psychotic break.

"It was, partially, but it didn't go all the way because you didn't have enough faith."

Grrr. There was that accusation again: not enough faith.

After that session and another one, she still said I was not completely well. I was flying to meet my parents and Linda for Christmas the next morning, and she offered a final session so I "would have a good vacation." I was put off by that. To me, it was in my hands whether or not I would have a good trip, not hers. I initially accepted the appointment, but later in the evening I changed my mind and cancelled it.

I was reading that night from a book about alternative medicine. It described a process called siphoning, which consists of pulling energy out of a person with the left hand and channelling it away by extending the other arm out and away from the body—almost exactly as I had done with Francois Leonard! I was speechless. Somehow I had unconsciously acted that out. Even though I could not deny being out of control, perhaps I had not been as dangerously so as I had seemed.

Christmas and New Year's was spent happily with family, and then it was time to return to Montreal and get back to work. Based on my previous year's performance, I earned an outstanding rating at my job. This time I knew I had earned it.

Later that spring, I was browsing in a bookstore when I discovered a remarkable spiritual book. It involved an exposition of truth, as well as the author's own enlightenment experience. With excitement over what I found I voraciously read the book several times. I ordered the author's other books over the Internet and waited eagerly for them to arrive. I felt I had discovered the most profound truth I had ever heard of. I felt thrilled and overjoyed.

After I read the books in early summer, I felt so sure of myself and how far I had come that I believed I didn't need my medication any more. Without consulting the doctor I abruptly stopped it. There were no side effects, and I felt really great and had a lot of energy. The one problem was a lack of ability to concentrate at my job. It was taking me longer to do things, and I made some foolish errors that caused delays. To me, it was a small price to pay for my newfound freedom. I was meditating and listening to spiritual music.

When I told my wife I was no longer taking my medication, she and Beatrice went on a month-long trip to Toronto to spend time with her family, but also because she didn't trust me that much. I spent the summer by myself, but I was very happy.

One day in late August, I was talking to my mother on the phone. She asked me whether I was still taking my medication, and I told her that I wasn't. "Oh, Robert, I'm worried," she said. She also said something negative about Linda. I was irritated at her and was afraid she would have a negative effect on my mental state if I saw her, so I cancelled Beatrice's first birthday party, which was coming up in a few weeks, because I didn't want my mother around.

Later on in the week, she called me to say that my sister's psychiatrist did not believe in false memories. He had taken her off some of her medications, and her memories of being sexually abused by Uncle Calvin came back. Inside, I felt an old sense of panic welling up again. The past was coming back to haunt me. My mom told me she hadn't been sure she should tell me because she didn't know if I could handle it. *Why did you tell me, then?* I wondered. I said, "You can still care about her but not necessarily decide whether the story is true or not."

"We believe her," my mom emphatically replied. There was little more to say. The conversation ended awkwardly, and then we hung up.

That night I had trouble sleeping. I was thinking I had to take a stand on this issue. I didn't believe the story that Uncle Calvin had sexually abused my sister. When the story first came up in 2002, I accepted it unquestionedly out of loyalty to my sister. Now, rationally considering the likelihood of this story, it seemed preposterous. It was a question of taking the word of my sister, who is not the most honest and sane person in the world, leaving aside the fact that she had been dabbling in tarot cards and Wicca and who-knows-what else, versus my uncle, whom I couldn't imagine even telling a lie, and who was a devout minister in a prominent Canadian church for all his adult life. I was certain this story was not true, and I realized I had to say so. It was my duty, since my reaction in 2002 had helped convince my parents of its validity. What I had learned from the spiritual teachings I had read was that it was necessary to stand up for the truth.

A series of altercations by e-mail was next. I received an angry e-mail from my sister. She attacked me for cancelling Beatrice's birthday party, saying that cancelling after my mom had made "one snarky comment" was a poor way to treat my parents after all they had done for Linda and me. She then continued to write that she was going through "a difficult time" and didn't want to have an argument with me. I was furious. I felt like I was being attacked by my mother with my sister's lies and then attacked by my sister with my mother's distortions. I decided to take them on together.

I forwarded the message to my parents, copying my sister, and added:

> I was wrong about what I said yesterday. It is not right to stand by and let an innocent man suffer slander! Uncle Calvin never molested anyone. He was an honest man, and it is my sister who is lying about the whole thing.

I said some other things that I don't remember clearly, but that was the gist of the message.

My father wrote back. Here is an excerpt of the message:

> Your sister is going through a difficult time right now. Please be respectful of her. Feel free to share the thoughts you are having with your psychiatrist, as well as any good thoughts you may have.

So that's it, I thought. *You're going to make it sound like it's me who's crazy and you and my sister are in the right.*

I wrote back:

> Sister: You are accusing a man who dedicated his life to serving God. Shame on you!

> Dad: You have the nerve to give me medical advice, so I have a question for you. How much excrement can a man swallow without being poisoned? Let me know; you seem determined to do it!

That evening I was feeling psychologically frail. I wanted some support, so I telephoned my brother.

"What's shakin'?" he said. My brother doesn't usually talk that way. From the way he'd answered, it was clear to me that he knew what was going on but didn't want to get involved. I jumped to that conclusion without asking. As soon as he said that, I didn't want to talk to him anymore. We only spoke for a minute.

Soon I received another email from my sister:

> You are a megalomaniac jerk!!!

She proceeded to tell me off or something; I didn't read the whole e-mail, I'm afraid, but I got the gist of it from the title. I replied to my sister, my parents and my brother as well:

> Nothing is shaking.

> No one who stands for the truth fights alone.

> I would rather die than agree with this lie ever again. I would rather die and pass into heaven than be part of this slander. No one who tells such wicked lies, and no one who spreads them, will ever be part of my family. I am happy to have good memories of Uncle Calvin back with me, and no one is going to taint them.

> Goodbye.

There were replies that followed that e-mail, but I didn't get a chance to read them. It was Monday, and I was going to work. I hadn't slept the night before. My wife needed the car, so she was dropping me off at work. She could tell something was wrong with me.

"What's wrong, honey? Tell me what's bothering you."

"It's my parents and my sister. They're telling lies about Uncle Calvin, the same lies that came up before. I'm so mad!" I became more agitated as I explained the situation. My voice was shaking.

"Take the day off work, honey." Then she asked a question that pushed me even further: "Why don't you take your medication?"

With that, I became furious at her too. I felt like she was implying that I was wrong because I was so worked up and was trying to medicate away the stand I was taking. I was ready to take a stand with her too, to push things right to the limit. No one seemed to understand that outrage at this wickedness really was appropriate.

"Let me out of the car," I said to her. I got out of the car and started walking away. I took off my wedding ring and threw it at the car. She and Beatrice drove away, and I walked in the opposite direction. I decided to go and visit the author who had written the spiritual books I had been reading, but as I walked past my company, I decided that someone should warn the people there about slander, since I could see it attacking them as well. I went inside my company and wrote up a resignation letter, which I sent to everyone in the department. I offered my resignation, suggested the vice president should fire some people whom I named in the letter, stating that he himself should resign if he didn't know what to do, and that I would perhaps reapply someday as the head of Human Resources. Then I left the company premises.

As I resumed my walk to the bus station to go for my planned visit, I suddenly heard the author's voice in my head (I had heard him speak on an online radio show before). The voice said, "Go to work, get a job!"

I decided that now that my career and my marriage were over, there was nothing left for me to live for. I prayed to God to make me the patron saint of the bipolar. I decided to check myself into the mental ward again, to try to help others. I turned and walked in the opposite direction, toward the hospital. I threw away my glasses, my keys, and my wallet, which contained all of my IDs. I looked into the sun without blinking. As I was walking, suddenly I could feel the presence of something massive and evil and invisible looming ahead. It towered before me, as tall as the overpass over the highway I had to cross to get to the hospital. It communicated to me with fury: "You are going to get sodomized if you come here!"

I decided that if I was wrong, and I had falsely accused my sister, then that was what I deserved anyway. If not, I was ready to challenge this evil presence. I continued on, undeterred. I passed over the highway and continued on my way. After two angry encounters, one each with a cyclist on the sidewalk and an aggressive driver while crossing the road, I kept going.

I was mentally disoriented and lost my way. I took a wrong turn and ended up in a residential area. I walked through it for a while and then ended up in an industrial area. I was completely lost now and wanted a break from walking, so I went into an open field. The field was full of dandelions. I sat down.

Then I realized I was completely without form now and could emulate anything I wanted. A silent voice came to me: *Emulate Jesus Christ*. With that, the whole world caught fire.

The field, the earth, and the sky all showed me their creation by God, with His Signature upon each and every dandelion, each blade of grass. Light shone from them. A transmission of mind from Jesus Christ and the Buddha was coming to me. It had imprinted itself in the earth for thousands of years, and now it was coming to me.

At the same time, an intense burning pain came to my head;

the revelation was too much for me. It was killing me, but what a way to die! I had two olfactory hallucinations, one an intense sweet smell, and, separate and distinct yet arising simultaneously was a sulphurous burning smell. They were so strong, so poignant it was difficult to resist focussing on them.

A huge evil presence came again, reaching up from the ground high into the air. It was trying to dislodge the revelation. *The last moment, or forty days?* As it asked it was pushing and pulling at my spirit, trying to unbalance me. Meanwhile, the terrible agony continued. I decided that I was willing to accept the agony of this experience to bring this consciousness into the world. *Forty days it is!* replied the presence.

I lost control of my body and began to run toward the road. It might be more correct to say my body was run like an inanimate object. A trailer truck was driving down the road (or was it only idling?). I leaped up on the cab of the truck and hooked my arm onto the side-view mirror. The truck stopped and the driver got out. I fell to the ground. I couldn't speak. The light of the sun was causing me excruciating anguish, and I had to get out of it. I crawled under the trailer, where it was mercifully dark.

A short time later police and paramedics arrived and pulled me back out into the light. I was willing to die but not to give up on the consciousness I was experiencing. I tried to communicate telepathically to the policeman: *Please shoot me! The agony is too much! You can tell everyone I went for your gun. No one will blame you.* I couldn't understand what the policeman and paramedics said; I didn't hear. The truck driver turned to go. I decided that if he would give up on me, I would give up too. I turned my eyes to the sun and exhaled deeply. He changed his mind and stayed until they put me in the ambulance.

In the ambulance, the paramedics gave me some medication. Suddenly I realized what I had written in my resignation letter that morning. Guilt stabbed me like a knife into my belly when I remembered my betrayal. Again it stabbed when I thought about a second person I had betrayed in the resignation letter. These reactions were experiential, not intellectual or emotional. Then I lost consciousness for a few minutes.

At the Hospital

Once at the hospital I was wheeled into the emergency room. My arm was bandaged from where I had fallen. The nurses asked me questions, but I did not feel like speaking. Eventually I told them my name so they could book me into the hospital. Then it was time for another psychiatric evaluation.

"Tell me what's going on with you, Robert."

Somehow I knew the psychiatrist's first name. "Louise, my whole family is slandering my Uncle Calvin and saying he abused my sister. I stood up to them, and they shamed me for it. Isn't that terrible?"

"No, not really," she answered with a smile.

Hearing that, I knew she was not someone who was honest, doctor or not. I turned my head away from her and refused to speak any further.

"Robert? Robert?" she tried, but I was finished with her. She went away.

I was taken upstairs and assigned to a room on the psychiatric ward. My roommate was an unsavoury character who dressed in black from head to toe, with skulls on his shirt. I tried to be friendly and held out my hand. "Hi, I'm Robert," I said.

"Tell me, Robert: did you do that to yourself?" he accused angrily, pointing to my arm.

I was surprised and taken aback. I didn't answer.

Later he asked if he could use my top dresser drawer to store some of his clothes. I agreed. The clothes were all black and creepy looking.

I was lying on my bed when another silent message came to me: *The wolf in sheep's clothing must be avoided at all costs.* Immediately I got up to leave the room.

The roommate, who was lying on his bed, seemed disturbed

that I was leaving. He called, "Hey, man, what's your name again? Hey, man?"

I didn't answer and left.

Eventually I had to come back for bedtime. I couldn't sleep that night either. I could hear my roommate listening to something on his earphones. I was beginning to have suspicions about him. Who knew what kind of gross music he was playing and what effect it was having on me subliminally?

I began to think about my family. I thought back to a night about a week earlier when I had thrown out a toy my sister had given to Beatrice. I felt it was a poisoned gift and wanted it gone. After I had gotten rid of it, I felt unsure as to whether I had done the right thing. Beatrice had come to me and had given me a hug.

"Ah, she tried to warn him," my roommate said quietly. I felt panicked. Could this wicked man read my mind, and was he warping it? I tried not to think about anything for the rest of the night, and again I couldn't sleep.

The next morning I felt this couldn't go on. I got up to go to the washroom. On my way back, I received another silent message: *The wolf in sheep's clothing must be defeated at all costs!* I came back to the room and moved his stuff out of my drawer. I let him know I wasn't afraid of him, and laughed at him, tweaking his toe as I was passing by his bed on the way to my own.

"You're going to get in trouble today, f---!" he said furiously, and got up and went out.

The nurse came in with my medication and breakfast. I was praying to get rid of this evil presence, and I decided that I would not eat or drink anything that day. It is written that to be rid of some evils a person needs to fast, and I wasn't sure where taking medication came down on this, so I decided not to take that either.

The nurse was very angry and said, "Suit yourself, Robert." I figured the hospital staff was coming to medicate me, so I decided to play a joke. I put the tray of food under my bed.

Sure enough, they restrained and medicated me. After that, the doctor and the nurse came back in. The nurse said in a smug way that Linda and Beatrice were safe in Toronto, as though I was a dangerous person who had been neutralized. I knew that what would keep them safe was to stand up to the evil that was hovering around, and I was prepared to do it.

The doctor asked me why I was not eating.

"I am above food today. Do you want me to prove it?"

"Stop trying to be funny," she replied. "I can see the tray of food under your bed. Who do you think you are, anyway?"

"Today I am Moses," I replied. I meant it figuratively, as I was going to make a stand. It probably wasn't the smartest thing to say to a psychiatrist, but I hadn't slept for many days and was mentally disorganized.

"Ah," said my roommate from the other side of the curtain, as though a sudden revelation. Apparently he had been listening.

After a short talk, the nurse and psychiatrist left. I fell into a blissful, dreamless sleep that lasted all day and night.

After the medication wore off, I woke up and my roommate was gone. He came back the next week and said to me, "I'm back …" in a way that I thought was supposed to scare me, but I just turned away and ignored him. He left for good the same day.

The rest of my hospitalization stay was uneventful. The doctor prescribed a fairly high dosage of medication, to be slowly tapered off through the fall. Linda and my father-in-law came to pick me up, at which time we had a meeting with my psychiatrists, the one from the hospital and my outpatient psychiatrist. They advised Linda that she should leave me if I stopped taking my medication again. It was at this time that I realized that I had forced Linda into a terrible decision: she had to either stay with me when I was off medication because she loved me or leave with Beatrice to protect her. I decided I wouldn't force her to make such a decision, and I resolved to follow doctor's orders.

I made peace with my sister and my family. I told them that

we could have a truce if none of us mentioned Uncle Calvin and the allegations ever again. My mother came close to breaking the truce one time, but I warned her and she let it go.

I felt like I had faced down the evil and had driven it away, but it was not a final victory. I didn't consider myself cured. The bipolar illness hadn't been satisfactorily resolved. And after the incident in the field near the hospital, where I had experienced a revelation, I knew that I would never be the same again.

Chapter 5:
Fifth Hospitalization—Victory

> *My brethren, if any of you do err from the way of the truth, and someone converts him from his error, let him know that he who converts a sinner from the error of his way, shall save his soul from death and wipe out a multitude of sins.*
> —James 5:19–20 (Lamsa translation)

I was ready to go back to work at the start of December 2005, but I was told to stay home until January 2006. I was also required to be examined by the company doctor before being allowed to return to work. I felt unwanted, and I probably was, but I was lucky to still have my job after the ridiculous and shameful thing I had done. To make matters worse, there were layoffs at the company that fall while I was away, and everyone's morale was really low. That year, I got a terrible rating for my performance for the year, which stood to reason after missing four months, and the lack of success on the assigned research projects. There was a reorganization of personnel, and Ken was no longer my boss. My new boss was actually one of the people I had suggested should be fired, but he was noble enough not to hold it against me. Adjusting to work was difficult, and the work itself seemed rather pointless after everything I had experienced.

Through the spring, strange events started to happen. I remember one vividly. Linda and I were returning home from dinner. We got out of our car when a strange-looking man, about fifty years old and walking a dog wearing a muzzle walked past our house.

"Are you going in there?" he asked.

"Yes," Linda replied.

"She's a pretty witch," he said, and kept walking. Very creepy and strange.

I won't recount other events. Most I can't remember, and other ones I don't want to talk about. I became convinced I was under attack by evil forces. I wanted to fight them off and leave a good legacy for children to come in the world.

Late in the spring we made a trip to Niagara Falls. We went with Linda's sister and her husband and son. Linda's brother-in-law took us to a Buddhist temple, which was a new experience for me. I was not too interested in the Buddha statue, but on the other side of the large room was something I had never seen before. It was a large icon of a woman with grace and beauty. The statue had a swastika on her brow. I thought of how this swastika had been used by Nazis, yet here it still was with its undiminished holiness on the face of this bodhisattva. It seemed to me there was nothing she couldn't forgive. Maybe I was worthy of love and forgiveness too. Tears came to my eyes.

Back from vacation, on a day in June I decided to walk home from work. The temperature was 31°C (88°F) and humid. It was a half-hour walk, but I thought I could make it. When I was rounding the last block, I suddenly realized I was suffering from heat exhaustion and wasn't going to make it home. At the same time, I smelled a strong, sweet smell, the same one I had smelled in the field in September 2005. A thought came to me: *What you tolerate on Earth will be tolerated in heaven.* I knew this was a Bible passage, although I wasn't sure I had it exactly right, and I realized I needed to know the truth of it before I died.

I was about to sit on the pavement when along came Linda in our car. She had picked up Beatrice and was coming down our street. She stopped and let me into the air-conditioned comfort of the car. I was saved. Once we arrived home, I went upstairs, got down on my knees and thanked God for saving my life.

I had joined an online spiritual forum earlier in the spring. That evening, I put the following questions up for discussion:

- What you tolerate on Earth will be tolerated in heaven. T/F
- Do people of advanced consciousness have a duty to help others ward off demonic attacks?

I received a reply from one of the participants in the forum. He said that both statements were false. I sent a reply attacking him, saying he was a wolf in sheep's clothing and should be removed from the forum. I copied the administrator of the forum in the e-mail. The administrator of the forum replied, basically suggesting that I cease and desist. I sent another e-mail to the participant, which he replied to under a different name. This convinced me that he was partially possessed by a demon.

In the meantime, a second participant replied to my original discussion question. He said that the passage I was looking for was Matthew 16:19, where Jesus was speaking to Simon Peter, giving him the power to "bind" and "release" whatever he wanted in heaven as on Earth. He also referred me to Ephesians 6:11–20. I looked it up and thanked him for his input. As it said, I asked him to pray for me, and I would pray for him as well. Upon further reading, I found the passage Matthew 18:18, in which Jesus said to all his disciples: "Truly I say to you, whatever you bind on earth will be bound in heaven, and whatever you release on earth will be released in heaven." I decided that I would no longer tolerate demons running amok, and I would do my part to bind them, on Earth and in heaven.

I sent another e-mail, this time a group message to the first and second participants as well as to the administrator of the forum. I thanked the second participant for his prayers. I told the administrator that there was a something that needed to be removed, and I gave the name of first participant had given me in his second e-mail. I blessed the first participant in the first name he had given me, and then I commanded the unclean spirit to come out of him in Jesus Christ's name.

Events quickly came to a head after that. I couldn't handle the power that had been triggered. I tried to go to work the next day but had no ability to concentrate. I sat in my office until it was time to go home. Back at home, I learned that I had been kicked out of the online spiritual forum. I became suddenly paranoid and thought that the people on the forum were evil, as was the spiritual writer the forum was based on (the same author I described in chapter 4). On my desk I saw a ceramic statuette of two angels facing each other that my mother had given me, and a toy that had a skull on it. The skull represented open and undisguised evil, and the second represented more dangerous evil, evil masquerading as truth and goodness. I wanted to destroy them both in effigy. I believed evil people were coming to take me, and I just had time to accomplish this before they arrived. I took the two objects and asked my wife where our hammer was. As I went outside, I realized I shouldn't be messing around with this kind of thing, so I just let them drop there. The angels shattered into many pieces, but the skull was made of soft plastic so it survived. Beatrice saw my state and started to cry.

"I have to go get some milk for Beatrice," Linda said. "I'm going to take her with me."

I took no notice of this. I was not interested. As she left, I went down to the basement. I went to the furthest corner and saw a wire hanging down. I pulled on it as hard as I could and it snapped. There was only a dull thud, no spark. (I found out later it was only a low-voltage telephone wire.) I went upstairs and lost consciousness.

I was roused by two men, one dressed as a policeman. They both looked to me like angels or some kind of divine beings. The policeman particularly looked like a Buddha. I stood up and embraced him. I was being taken away by gods to the hospital.

But suffering continued as I witnessed the defilement of my inner being, moment by moment. I alternated between elation and despair.

At the Hospital

I was taken to the emergency room, bound hand and foot and across the chest, and with a cover over my mouth. I thought I was in hell, where I would be bound in darkness forever. No time passed. I had a vision of a dragon being cast into a lake of fire. No time passed. I tried to escape from the hell, but I could not.

Eventually the morning came, and with it the sun rose. I realized I was not in hell. Linda came to see me, and she was angry at me. I rebuked her in return and told her to go away.

The psychiatrist on duty quickly assessed me as being in the midst of another episode. Linda returned and told me she loved me. I saw her as a great beauty, with divinity and love shining from her face. I looked at her, and we both cried with love. She told me I was having another episode. I agreed and told her I was not going to get better this time.

Upstairs, I was assigned to the pink room right away and was told I mustn't leave the room for the time being. Maybe it was because of a lack of space, or maybe it was because I was so crazy. A nurse said to me, "Robert, you realize you have to take your medication." I saw a blue light in her eyes, and that was when I realized I didn't need to take it, so I refused. Why they didn't medicate me immediately is beyond me, but they didn't.

A new psychiatrist was assigned to me. It was a gift of grace.

I was convinced the world was going to end within four days or so. To make matters worse, the washroom adjoining the pink room was locked, and I was afraid other patients would get me in trouble if I left the pink room and I would be strapped down and medicated. A solution shortly arrived in the form of a carton of milk. I drank the milk, relieved myself in the empty carton, sealed it up and left it outside my room with the leftovers from lunch. Problem solved.

The next time I had to relieve myself, I was not so fortunate. I had too much to be able to close the carton again afterward, so I had to give it to a nurse. "Ugh," she said, and made a face, taking it away.

The orderlies came to see why I had done that. When they realized the washroom was locked, they unlocked it for me. "Thank you," I said.

"No, we thank you!" they replied.

A strange thing was found when my blood test results came back from the sample taken when I was admitted. My blood level of medication I had been prescribed was nil. The doctor confronted me with it, but I didn't know what happened because I had not decided to stop the medication before being hospitalized, and I thought I had been taking it, all except the last night when I was too disoriented to remember.

The nurses continually checked my blood pressure and asked me to take my medication, so I had to refuse it over and over. Late one night, when everyone else was asleep, I lay awake. I became excited and said, "I bind myself to God on Earth, and I bind myself to God in heaven." I realized that none of the other patients could bother me as long as I stayed in my room. Indeed, several of them had been trying to bother me since I was admitted, but they were completely powerless. I went out to the nurses' station.

"I need to use the phone," I said. I wanted to phone home and ask for a bible. (The phone that is available for patients was disconnected at mealtimes and overnight.)

The orderly came over. "Go back to your room."

"What's more important, following God's rules or following hospital rules?"

"Following hospital rules."

I was finished with him once he said that. I turned to the overnight nurse and made a strange gesture toward her and then went back to my room.

The next morning was the hospital staff's turn with me. Two orderlies and a nurse came and said I could take my pills orally or I could take an injection. I said I wasn't being given a choice. The nurse reiterated that I had a choice—I could either take the medication orally or by injection. After arguing back and forth, she agreed that I didn't have a choice. With that, I began to pull down my pants so they could give me the shot. (These shots are administered into the buttocks.)

"Whoa! Wait!" they exclaimed. The nurse had to go prepare the shot. As they left, I dropped my trousers and lay down on the bed, exposing my rear end for all to see. This was a message to the hospital staff! If you want to treat me like a piece of meat, go ahead! I won't pretend that you need my permission.

After they gave me the shot, I thanked each of them by name and shook their hands. No hard feelings, they were just doing their jobs.

One of the orderlies smiled and called me Casanova.

This was the only time they medicated me by force during this stay at the hospital.

As the week went on, my sanity began to return. I found I was quite creative and resourceful with what they gave me in terms of food and drink. I ate very small meals, only a small portion of what was served. During this week, Linda constantly visited me in the pink room. She stayed by my side and was a great comfort to me. By Saturday or so, I realized that the world was not going to end. I kept some of the insanity in my mind but shared little of it with others, which I think is what helped it subside.

After a week in the pink room I was placed in a regular room. I was still refusing all medication. I could tell I was no longer mentally ill, having regained my sanity and control over myself. I sent a note to my doctor:

> Dear Doctor:
> What do you find harder to believe, a faulty initial diagnosis or spontaneous remission of florid mania and psychosis within one week? Think it over ...
> I

On the downstroke of the pen where I had intended to write my name, the pen's ink stopped, so try as I might, I could only write "I". The significance of this bears explaining. From my readings of mystical literature, I had read that the highest level of human awareness is a state of identity, with no object, only the sense of "I". This is such closeness to God such that it is almost an overlap. By writing my name at the bottom of the message, it was tantamount to placing the origin of the healing from bipolar disorder within my limited self. When the pen would not write my name, and simply wrote "I" instead, it was a miracle asserting that the origin of the recovery was with God, and not me at all. It humbled me, while at the same time giving me confidence that the recovery was real.

A few days later my wife was visiting, and I told her I wanted to see my daughter. Linda agreed, and we asked a nurse about it. After consulting with the doctor, the nurse declared that I would not be allowed to see my daughter until I agreed to take my medication. I was very upset by this decision, but I didn't act out. I calmly told the nurse I would think about what to do next.

That night I decided I would not eat until I was allowed to see Beatrice. I sent a terse note to the doctor:

> Dear Doctor,
> I am unwilling to passively accept your refusal to allow me to see my daughter. I will not eat until further notice.
> Robert

The next day and the day after that I refused food. Honestly, I didn't expect the hospital staff to give in, and I wasn't prepared to give in either. I thought I was going to end up being force-fed, but that was not how it turned out. After two full days of fasting, my psychiatrist came to talk to me.

"What do you want, Robert?" she asked.

"I'm not sure if you're ready."

"You're not sure if you're ready?"

"No, I'm not sure if *you* are ready."

"Oh, I'm ready!" I could tell by the way she smiled that she was at a loss for what to do with me. We agreed that I would write up a note that evening, outlining what I wanted, and we would have a meeting the next morning.

That evening I wrote a note explaining my state of mind. I declared that I was no longer psychotic or manic and was, in fact, in a very relaxed state. I was seeing the beauty of life in a way that I had rarely done previously in my life. I stated that I wanted to be declared cured of bipolar disorder by the medical community and to go home with my wife and daughter. I apologized for my foolish words about my spiritual teacher, since I had told my doctor he was evil when I was in the pink room, and asked God to forgive me. I signed the letter and gave it to the nurses.

The next morning I had the meeting with the psychiatrist, a social worker and several nurses. The psychiatrist told me she had read some of the letter and said I needed to take my medication. She tried to persuade me to agree, but I did not. One good thing that was resolved at the meeting was that I would be allowed to see my daughter if I stopped fasting, to which I gladly agreed.

It was really great to see Beatrice again when we had our visit, but she wasn't that interested in visiting with me. I guess it was her two-year-old way of saying she didn't appreciate the time I had been away from her. Linda was getting impatient with the situation and told me, "If you don't take your medication, Beatrice and I are leaving!" I felt really trapped because I felt it was my duty to God not to take my medication, since I was not ill anymore. I felt I had to show the world how I had been cured, which wouldn't be possible if I was taking medication.

A family conference with my brother helped me to see the light. One afternoon, he and Linda came to visit and spoke to me about taking my medication. My brother said that although I could survive in the protected sphere of the hospital, it didn't mean I would be able to function outside it. I knew that this was false, and I told him so. The hospital environment was actually fairly adverse to me, with patients who were unpredictable and sometimes hostile for no reason, apart from the unpleasantness of being incarcerated against one's will.

Then my brother said something that really got through. "I think the problem is with too much of one extreme or another. You need to find a middle way."

I found this to be something of a miracle—to hear my brother, who is not very religious, almost verbatim quoting the Buddha. This suddenly convinced me that I needed to take my medication. I went to speak to the nurses and told them I would take my medication that evening. I realized that the cure of bipolar disorder had already been achieved and there was nothing left to prove. Adopting a "macho" attitude toward my medication did not serve me, nor did it serve anyone else. Taking my medication would be an act of great love and sacrifice for those around me.

I was prescribed a fairly low dose of medication, and within a few weeks I was released from the hospital. I don't think the psychiatrist fully understood what had been accomplished, nor her helpful role in the process. She told me I was being discharged because there were sicker patients who needed a place on the ward, so she was letting me go home. She also thought I was a risk for stopping my medication. In my prognosis, she wrote: reserved. Funny, the first time I read it, I thought it said: reversed. I would settle for that.

After I was released from the hospital, I wrote a letter to my parents. I wrote that I had wanted to stand up for the truth the year before, but I became hostile and confrontational because of the guilt I felt. I felt guilty because I had helped to convince them of the veracity of the sexual abuse story. I detailed that I was certain I had never been sexually abused by Uncle Calvin, and that I remembered him as a nice man. I said I would welcome any response to the letter they would choose to make, whether as a letter, a phone call or silence.

Epilogue

It has now been more than five years since my last episode of bipolar disorder. I can tell that the illness is gone. I am still taking my medication, and I no longer feel any side effects. I had a big problem with "putting a bandage over an infected wound," but now that this wound of bipolar disorder has healed, a cosmetic bandage does no harm. It is definitely worth it to keep peace in my family.

Linda and I had another child, our son, Samuel, in 2007. He and Beatrice are a great blessing in our lives. Life passes with joy, every day bringing new adventures and new challenges, which we face with love, hope and faith. There are still lots of ups and downs, but we get through them.

Part 2
TRANSCENDING BIPOLAR DISORDER

Foreword

To open this section, I think it appropriate to reiterate that I am neither a doctor nor a psychologist. For help in dealing with an illness like bipolar disorder, the services of a professional would be of great assistance. My advice cannot be taken as medical nor psychological advice. By contrast, I would also posit that my experience is extremely valuable, since I am a case where recovery has taken place, leading from a state of having five episodes in four years to a state where no episodes have taken place in more than five years (and counting). This is a case that can teach people something extremely valuable, and I want to share everything I can about it.

As you read this section, it would be most valuable to question whether what I say is true for you and makes sense to you. Discard any information that doesn't seem right to you. If you feel something is valid, or even obvious, you should know that it will not have power in your life unless you live it. For example (to anticipate something coming later in the text), forgiveness would be nice and may be obvious as a strategy—but are you really going to *do* it, or not? Getting to a place of joy and peace does not involve passing a set of true or false or multiple choice questions but by coming into harmony with divine principles.

Chapter 6:
Newly Diagnosed with Bipolar Disorder

The time following diagnosis of bipolar disorder was a huge shock for me. I initially went into denial, refusing to accept what the doctor was telling me. It was a life sentence to me, especially as the doctor presented it. With what you will learn from this book, bipolar disorder does not have to be seen that way anymore, but it is a serious condition that will require changes.

Here are some strategies that worked really well for me:

- *Avoiding sugar, at least initially.* I pay attention to how the foods I eat make me feel. I found that sugar especially gave me a "something is wrong" kind of panicky feeling shortly after I ate it. It may be worth trying to cut it down, or eliminate it from your diet for a while, and see if you feel better. If you feel better, leave it out. Lately I find that sugar doesn't affect me adversely the way it used to, so I have let it back into my diet. If it does bother me, I have come to learn that this sensation is just a physical one, and I don't give any importance to the feeling it produces.

- *Avoiding illegal drugs and excessive alcohol consumption.* One or two drinks may be harmless from time to time, but it is not good to drink excessively. Illegal drugs should be eliminated completely. Your mind is fragile right now; treat it right! If you can't resist the urge for these substances, seek help from Alcoholics Anonymous or another recovery group specific for the substance abuse problem you have.

- *Getting exercise.* If you are being medicated with a fairly high dosage, you might feel like you have little energy. Even still, it is good to get some light exercise, such as walking. If you feel up to it, something more vigorous would be good, like jogging. I find that getting exercise gives me a natural high, as long as I don't overdo it. It is easier to maintain if it is something that you enjoy, such as I found with jogging.

Swimming is worth trying too. When I was depressed I made a liberating discovery. I went swimming at the local pool, and as soon as I got into the water, the depression lifted. Unfortunately, as soon as I came out of the pool, I felt depressed again, but at least I had a temporary respite.

- *Be gentle with yourself.* If your experience is like mine, you have done some things you are not proud of or are even downright ashamed of. Don't let yourself focus on behaviour you are ashamed of that you committed when you were not yourself. This is self-indulgent and won't make you feel any better. If you regret some of your past behaviour, accept that it was part of the illness and forgive yourself. If appropriate, it may be worthwhile to apologize to anyone you have hurt and then put your attention elsewhere.

Being gentle with yourself also means giving yourself time to rest. If you are exhausted, just go ahead and sleep for a while. Don't hold yourself to rigorous performance standards for the next few weeks. Take it easy. Now is a good time to stop judging yourself harshly, if you have a habit of doing so.

Chapter 7:
Some Thoughts on Hypomania, Mania and Psychosis

Hypomania

One feature of hypomania is the presence of grandiose thoughts. These thoughts are tantalizing because they actually have a small grain of truth to them. The truth is that you really are great! You are great like you think you are. The lie in the thoughts is that you are better, greater, somehow beyond others. Everyone has the greatness of being created by God; I do, you do, and so does everyone else. For that matter, so do the plants, animals, and everything you share the earth with. The Bible tells us that we are the stewards of the plants and animals. God is our Master—conduct yourself with the knowledge that you are accountable.

You have a surge of energy and creativity: What are you going to do with it? As you sow, so shall you reap. Making the best of your abilities, trying to make the world a better place is fantastic. Working toward your own greatness for your own aggrandizement is not. Stay humble. Pray for humility before your pride is humiliated. Pursuing fame and wealth for their own sake will lead to trouble.

I have a friend who sleeps only five hours a night, and he has done so for many years. He is a high-performing individual, accomplishing a huge amount of work each day. He works hard but also has many friends and a loving wife. Even though he is sometimes irritable, people are drawn to him because of his high energy and general friendliness. He is passionate about his work, feeling that he is helping humanity through his efforts. He is not discouraged by obstacles in his work. He doesn't talk about it much, but I would say that the source of his energy is love, and it stops him from going astray. As a result, he doesn't seem to be in any danger of going too far, into mania or psychosis. I see him as a good example of what is possible when one is motivated by love.

Mania and Psychosis

From my experience, the best place for someone who has crossed over into mania and psychosis is a hospital. It is pointless to try to reason with such a person or to try to "figure them out." The most important thing is to make sure they don't hurt themselves or anyone else. Hospitalization is what is needed. I write this for the sake of those who are in the position to call emergency medical staff to take the person to the hospital, not for the person in such a state themselves, who, realistically, is not in a position to listen. The hospital staff will make a decision whether the sufferer needs medication, whether voluntarily or involuntarily if they refuse, or whether they just need time to come down to earth on their own.

A Model of Healing from Psychosis

A psychosis starts when an "insane" thought is held in the mind, and it is believed with conviction. This insane thought then leads to insane corollaries. Consider it as a circle whose diameter is expanding (see diagram 1 below). Rather than attacking the root insane thought that is at the centre (which is bound to be unsuccessful because the thought is so firmly entrenched), one continues to hold loving thoughts, and if possible, to carry out loving behaviours guided by spiritual principles. These thoughts and behaviours are intrinsically contrary to the expansion of the "sphere" of insanity, since love takes one in the diametrically opposite direction from insanity. This make the diameter of insanity contract (see diagram 2 below), but *without opposition of the core insane thought*. Eventually the sphere shrinks completely, and all that's left is the insane thought at the root. At this time the root thought will be questioned and spontaneously reversed. I remember the instant my mind said, "Hey, maybe this thought is not true," and with that, it was gone.

Central core insane thought

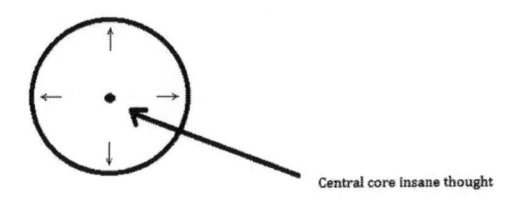

Diagram 1. From central insane thought, insanity progresses.

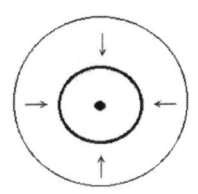

Diagram 2. Shrink insanity without attacking central core insane thought, by utilizing spiritual principles to govern thought and action

In my case I had been trying to implement spiritual principles and had been reading spiritual literature before the last psychosis occurred, while taking medication. It may not be successful to try to teach such principles to an individual already in a state of psychosis. Antipsychotic medication administered by a doctor as a stop-gap intervention would most likely be an important first step in healing in such a case.

This strategy can be seen as a way of "binding" the psychotic thought, rendering it more and more powerless. The "cure" is something that comes as a natural, indirect consequence.

Chapter 8:
Dealing with and Overcoming Depression

Introduction

When you feel depressed, it is part of the phenomenon to feel that the sensation is permanent. Everything is telling you that you will never get better. Realize that this is part of the illness speaking. Tell yourself out loud: "This will pass." While it is true that not everyone recovers from any illness in question, for most people, depression passes. The clouds lift, and the sun shines again. This section analyzes elements of depression and strategies to transcend them.

Talk to your doctor about medication. If you have very low energy, you may be overmedicated. This was a factor in my depression in 2002. Conversely, although I do not have experience with them, antidepressants have helped many people recover from depression.

There were six key factors in my depression in 2002. As you read them, think about how many of them are present in your situation.

1. *The belief everyone would desert me.* When I was depressed, it brought out a deep-seated fear of being abandoned. I was afraid everyone would leave me: my wife, my friends, and I was afraid I would be fired from my job. When I was in this negative state, I was having a negative influence on those around me. I would "drag them down," so to speak. It was only when they became really sad, upset or angry that I would snap out of it for a few minutes, mustering enough energy to elevate my mood.

This belief turned out not to be based on reality. No one abandoned me through my two-month depression. My wife and my family stood by me, friends asked about my health and my job was waiting for me when I was ready to return.

Take a look at your own life. See who is standing by you right now. Make a list of everyone, whether friends, family, coworkers or health-care professionals. Don't cancel anyone off the list if they are complaining about you somewhat—can you blame them? The important thing is that they are still there with you. Thank each one of them in turn in person, by phone or by e-mail. They haven't given up—thank them for it and tell them you won't give up either and that you are trying to get back up. Gratitude is a great antidote to depression. See whether this will lift your spirits, at least temporarily.

2. *The belief I was being treated unfairly by the universe.* I felt that terrible suffering was being inflicted on me for no good reason. The whole issue of sexual abuse by Uncle Calvin raised the belief that life was unfair. How could this be allowed to happen?

Ultimately I believe that life will turn out to be fair. Sometimes a long view is needed. The issues of life may not be resolved within a lifespan of eighty or so years, but I believe in God's final justice. Some things have to be left up to that. Aside from this, there remains the question of whether these allegations were even true. As I described in Part 1, I have come to believe with conviction that they were not. In retrospect, what I had wanted turned out not to be justice but the fulfilment of fantasies that were not based in reality!

Do you feel you are being treated unfairly? What is unfair to you? Write a list. Ask yourself about each one of these in turn: Am I sure I understand the true nature of this situation? What if what I believe is not true? Even if it is true, the best thing might be to trust the universe to sort it out for the justice of everyone, in its own time.

Here's an example: A loved one died, even though he or she had led a good life or was too young to die. This person didn't deserve this. It wasn't fair.

How do you know where your loved one is? The body is gone, but was that all you cared about? Wasn't it something more than just "meat" that you loved? Where is his or her spirit now? Can you honestly be sure it has been permanently extinguished? Why not believe he or she is somewhere else now. Say a prayer. You will always miss the person if you loved him or her, but it doesn't have to be an agonizing, soul-crushing regret. You will join your loved one someday; believe that instead.

3. *The belief I was on a downward spiral, and the future would only be worse.* Despite how bad I felt, I was convinced that it was just the start of something worse. I have already described how I thought everyone would desert me. I thought I would be unable to work and have to go back to living with my parents, which I didn't want (and I am sure they didn't want either!). I was still coping with the belief that I would be forced to take medication for the rest of my life, which I didn't want.

If you have come to believe that you can predict your future from now until the end of your life, I have some good news—you can't! No one knows where they will be one day from now. Your depression could lift before you know it, no matter how long you have suffered from it.

Think about whether there is anything you can do that would make a difference, giving your life more integrity, making your life more the way you wanted it to be at more idealistic times in your life, living up to your dreams of yourself. For me, the decision to not take my antidepressants helped me stop being depressed (note that I had not started them, I was refusing to take them). For you, perhaps giving up on pride and taking your medication would help. Search your mind for something you could do to turn the direction you are moving.

4. *The belief I was a broken man.* Leading up to my depression, I'd had a series of adverse experiences. I had been forced to take medication. I had been forcibly restrained. I had experienced the inability to perform at my workplace. Perhaps most damaging of all, I had experienced the loss of my sanity. These experiences broke my pride and a good portion of my self-esteem. I had wished death would take me, although I didn't want to do it myself.

It turned out I was temporarily "broken," but I've come back together again. It is true that as a result of my experiences, I can no longer look at the world the way I did before, but this is true in a good way. I see a greater wholeness in life and a greater potential to interact in powerful ways with the world. I had never given much thought to bipolar disorder or psychosis, and now, here I am, nine years later, writing about my experiences and trying to help others with the condition. The road can take a person in any kind of unexpected direction.

If you feel broken, and if you are broken, you just have to believe that you can be put back together again, in a new and exciting way. If your situation is like mine, you may not be able to envision it right now. You simply must have faith and courage to see you through the ordeal. Talking to others, especially a psychologist who is compassionate and caring, will help. Some days are bad enough that you just have to live through them.

5. *The belief I had lost my identity.* Prior to my illness I saw myself as a tough, no-nonsense, hard-boiled chemist. When it struck, every part of that definition was threatened. The whole world didn't look the way it had before, and I knew I was different. My own weakness shocked me. The strangeness of the world shocked me. I believed my professional abilities had gone and would never return. I never recovered my former identity.

   On the other hand, I have gained a new identity, one that fosters much greater happiness and joy than the old one did. I see myself as someone who adopts as many positive spiritual traits as possible and tries to let go of limiting ones. I believe in my ability to change while at the same time doing my best to hold onto the virtues I have tried to adopt, such as compassion, empathy and love.

   As an interesting aside, a spiritual teacher named Ramana Maharshi proposed a method of self-inquiry whereby students consistently ask themselves, "Who am I?" By following this practice, students eventually discover enlightenment.

   Who are you, anyway? Maybe you aren't who you thought you were. If you are depressed now, your true nature certainly isn't who you think you are now. Go deeper and find out who you really are. You have the power to shape your personality.

6. *God wanted me to experience depression so that I could show others how to get out of it.* Being caught in a state of depression is more than just a bad mood or an unpleasant experience. It felt like something had caught hold of my spirits and was pressing down on me. I believe there is truth to this sensation and it was not just imagination. I believe that, in some cases at least, there are dark forces at work when a person becomes depressed. These dark forces

want nothing better than for you to stay depressed as long as possible, even for you to give up on life, even to commit suicide. And I say to you: *fight them*! Now is a good time to ask for God's help. If you are a Christian, pray in Jesus Christ's name if you can.

Try this prayer: *Dear God, I pray that you will dispel these dark forces from my life, in Jesus Christ's name. AMEN.*

Another spiritual exercise to try is to simply chant "OM" (rhymes with foam). It is a common "mantra" used in meditation. This is a good exercise because it is not intellectual or conceptual, so your mind will not get in the way. Don't be fooled by its simplicity—it is powerful. In Hinduism, OM is considered one of the names of God. Repeat it slowly and rhythmically, and watch the demons flee!

CHAPTER 9:
Transcending Bipolar Disorder: Strategies and Exercises

Some Opening Comments

If you want to transcend bipolar disorder, you first have to accept and understand that it will require you to change your thoughts and personality. Many of the thoughts and attitudes you have now are, frankly, those of a mentally ill personality. If you don't want to make such changes, you can live the life you had before, with medication. If the condition worsens with time, however, or medication doesn't help, and you want to reverse the progression of the illness, you first have to be willing to change. For me, the illness itself was sufficient motivation to change. Change takes work, but know that it is completely worthwhile for its own sake. Indeed, you may finally become grateful that you had the illness if it is what finally helps you to change in the way that has always been possible.

Don't stop your medication without consulting a doctor. It will take time for these practices to become part of who you are, to become ingrained in you. The length of time depends upon you. The suggestions and tips I am giving you are not a substitute for taking medication. If you are highly prone to relapse, any single large piece of unfinished business may be enough to trip you up and put you into the hospital if your mind is not protected with medication. If you ever do decide to stop your medication, do so with the help of a psychiatrist, taking his or her advice throughout. Realize that taking medication does not necessarily make you a weak person, nor does going without medication necessarily make one a holier or stronger person.

Here is something else to think about. It is an expression commonly bandied about: "What goes around comes around." Similarly, "If you send out negative energy, it comes back to you." While this is true in principle, I have seen that it is not always exactly when we are doing wrong that we experience negative consequences. Sometimes these consequences are delayed. Furthermore, when I attempted to change my ways and reform, I experienced immediate negative consequences. If you are in the grip of negativity, you may expect you will have to "pay for it," in a small fraction at least, to get out of the grip.

Mottos and Their Strength

What are the current mottos that you live by? You might at first think you do not have any, but this is not the case; everyone lives by something. Do you understand that you can change your whole life with the thoughts you choose? Some thoughts are weakening, others empowering. Some thoughts, adopted as a motto to live by, can, with time, reshape your whole life in a powerful new way, letting you break through to new heights of existence.

There are two important mottos I adopted along my spiritual path. I wholeheartedly recommend them.

- *Be kind to all of life, and always be forgiving.* I started following this motto in 2005. I found that it took a lot of practice to develop into a consistent habit. I was starting from a base where I was not consistently kind and often held grudges over petty events. I began a habit of taking some time toward the end of each day, perhaps a half hour, and searching my mind for instances where I was not forgiving. I made the commitment to letting resentment go each time I sensed it. After a period of several months, the process began to become ingrained in me, so something felt wrong if I was holding even minor resentments. I could feel the disturbance inside myself and knew I had work to do. After maintaining this practice, the instances of needing to forgive occurred less and less frequently. At first they happened every day or so, later much less often. Now I find that resentments hardly ever occur, and if they do, I let go of them easily and almost without effort.

- *Honour all men.* The second motto, to honour all men and women, was like a shield I kept at the ready, to prevent me from acting in inappropriate fashion. I'd read it in the Bible (1 Peter 2:17) in 2006 and maintained it as my attitude throughout my fifth and final hospitalization. As I followed this practice I was prepared to be patient and polite, treating others with respect and honour no matter how they acted toward me initially or in return. Knowing my commitment to do this gave me courage, strength and faith in a positive outcome in the midst of adversity. This motto is an excellent antidote to feelings of grandiosity. While it is actually true that you also deserve honour, you may or may not receive it. Regardless, if you are prepared to honour others as they deserve, you will reap the benefit: others will come to respect you in many cases, and even if they don't, you will not have lowered yourself to their level by being rude in return while developing a mutually negative relationship with another being.

The thoughts you live by can be likened to different kinds of engines. Some thoughts are very weak, like a toy car, and if that is all the power you own, you can be stopped just as easily. Other thoughts are like an unstoppable tank engine, and if you adopt them, you will become just as strong, breaking through tougher and tougher barriers on your way to your ultimate destination. The only question is how you want to live; you choose to be strong or weak.

While these two mottos are powerful and worked wonders for me, you can use your own mottos that work for you. If you want to choose your own, be sure to pick something that is loving and apply it to all parts of your life. Spiritual passages from the scriptures of various religions would be completely suitable. If you are already part of a religion, feel free to use something from it. Keep it short and simple so your mind can easily retain it.

The Power of Forgiveness

Forgiveness opens the doors that lead to many blessings. It is our power as human beings and our birthright from God. Here is an exercise in forgiveness. Try it out and see how much lighter you feel.

An Exercise in Forgiveness

1. Make a list of everyone who has hurt, wronged or made trouble for you, as far back as you can remember. Include everyone you can think of.

2. Ask yourself whether you can forgive each one in turn. Concentrate on your spiritual heart, at the centre of your chest, as you do this. Take a few minutes and breathe deeply. For each person you can forgive, cross the name off of your list. If there are no more names, go on to step 5.

3. Think about how each person left on the list has wronged or harmed you. What was the negative result of this? For example, if someone you trusted took advantage of you and now you feel suspicious, can you see that this is a choice you are making now, in the present, by holding on to a grudge? If you forgive him or her, you could regain your openness. Whatever this person did to you is in the past. You make your present and future. If that helps you forgive, cross some more names off of the list. If the names are all crossed out, go on to step 5.

4. For each name left on the list, write beside it the name of someone *you* have wronged in the past, whether earlier

in the day or many years ago. If you don't have enough new names to match up with your list of "victimizers," use the same new names more than once. Agree to forgive in exchange for being forgiven for what you have done wrong. Are you willing to forgive under these conditions? If not, do you understand that you won't be forgiven for what you have done wrong if you won't do this? This is a painful path.

He abused me, he beat me, he defeated me, he robbed me—in those who harbour such thoughts hatred will never cease. He abused me, he beat me, he defeated me, he robbed me—in those who do not harbour such thoughts hatred will cease.

—Words of the Buddha, from *the Dhammapada*

5. When all the names are crossed out, you are finished! Take the list and tear it up and throw it away, or better yet, burn it! Welcome to a life of being forgiven, of forgiving and being unburdened. Congratulations and God bless you! Now it is a matter of maintaining this state of mind.

Dealing with Fear/Terror

Fear is part and parcel of bipolar disorder and can run very deep. Fears can be dealt with, even if they are so intense that they can be called terror. Here are some guidelines for dealing with fear.

- Pay attention to how you are breathing. If you are very frightened, your breathing is probably very shallow and perhaps irregular. Breathe deeply and evenly, even if this requires all of your attention.
- If the fear is really intense, don't bother to think up clever counterarguments. You probably won't be able to convince yourself.

- Relax your body and let the fear pass through you. Don't fight it. Bring faith to your fears, and tell yourself you are in God's Hands no matter what happens. Force yourself to sing a song, a spiritual one of faith if you know any. Give this step several minutes. If you feel even a little better, continue the practice.

If all of these don't work, pray to God and tell Him how afraid you are and that you need His help. Surrender to whatever happens. Try to pray with all the intensity of the terror you are feeling; scream if you have to. The intensity matters more than the words you use. Accept what comes as His answer. Keep trying until you get through.

When It's Hard to Get Going: The Thymic Thump

If you find it hard to wake in the morning or are lacking energy during your day, there is a fifteen-second exercise that can help you. It is called the "thymic thump." For this exercise, you need to know that the thymus gland is located at the middle of the chest, just below the breastbone.

- Make a fist with your left hand.
- Think of someone you love, or a pet. If you don't have a pet and you don't love anyone, think of me. (That's a joke, but it might work …)
- Thump the thymus firmly but gently three times. As you do, say "ha" with each thump.
- Repeat three times.

Without getting into the alternative medicine technicals, the thymic thump reenergizes your body and can lift your spirits, too. Your willpower will shoot up, and your enthusiasm will be back. It sounds deceptively simple, but it works. Try it and see!

Dealing with "Attacks"

In the course of your life, you, like anyone else, will have many experiences. Most are typical, normal experiences that anyone can relate with. I am going to tell you about a few "strange and abnormal" experiences I had, and how I successfully handled them.

The first one I will describe was when I was hospitalized for the last time. I was in the psych ward hallway, and another patient came by to talk to me. She seemed pleasant enough. I spoke with her for a minute, and then suddenly she said something in a low, seductive voice about "unclean spirits" and waved her hand toward me. I had a sensation of energy brushing against my hip. Immediately, I turned on my heel and walked away from her without saying another word. She turned and began to follow me, but I told her to go away and leave me alone. It is really important not to mess with that kind of stuff!

Another incident happened during the same hospitalization. A woman with a very unpleasant demeanour came up to me. She began to chant in a rhythmic way while glaring at me, and it was disturbing. I responded by chanting "OM" back to her, but without aggression or emotion. Immediately, I could feel a sort of turbulence in the air. She stopped directing her attention toward me and focussed on someone else instead.

The important thing to understand is that you don't need to get involved in these affairs. Just walk away, or at most, stand your ground, but you don't need to "fight to win" against these things. It's up to God to sort out these things. This is one area where curiosity and desire to understand work against you if you let it. Give this stuff a wide berth!

The Influence of What You Surround Yourself With

- *Music.* Music can have a profound effect on our moods, simultaneously impacting us on several levels. The words have an impact, and so does the music itself. This can give results for good or for ill. I have always greatly enjoyed music, but the type of music I like has changed throughout the years. When I was younger, I liked popular music but also hard rock. I now understand that hard-rock music, with few exceptions, has a negative effect on my life force. It often contains negative lyrics, put together with a negative musical background. If you love yourself, donate this "music" to a garbage can near you!

There are all kinds of music that have a beneficial effect on moods. To name a few: Jazz, soul, country, classical, religious. Pop music is often okay, but there is an edge of negativity to it at times. I would avoid rap music too.

A general piece of advice I can give you is to stay away from negative music. If you are away from it for a while and hear it again, you will know how draining it can be. If you are like me, you will really want to turn it off when you hear it. If you are immersed in its influence, you might initially have to take my word about its effects. The question you need to ask yourself is not whether there are any exceptions to the rule of people being negatively affected by such music as hard rock, but whether it affects you negatively.

- *Television and Movies.* Television and movies are a place where there is a lot of negativity. Avoid television and movies that contain violence. Personally, I don't watch a lot of television—I would much rather read a good book. If you love movies, look into older movies to see some real classics.

- *Computer and Video Games.* If you want to feel better, this is an obvious place to cut. Many computer and video games get you involved in simulated mayhem and violence, for which you are rewarded in some way. Even most simulation games have a negative undertone, where the milieu is set against you and you have to overpower it. If you want to be a kinder person, let it all go. I am speaking from experience here. I used to play computer games constantly, and I really liked some of the most evil games out there. I feel like I didn't come away unscathed from this, although I have recovered now that I don't play and haven't for many years. You will feel much "cleaner" if you stop playing. The only computer games I can recommend are games like chess, or card games (but not gambling games).

Meditation on the Spiritual Heart

When bipolar disorder happens, there is an imbalance in the energies of the heart. Here is an exercise to help the spiritual heart.

- Sit comfortably, with your spine erect. Close your eyes, and breathe slowly and deeply.
- Concentrate on your spiritual heart, which is in the centre of your chest at the same level as your heart.
- Put your hands palms together with your fingers extended. Put your joined hands over your spiritual heart, with the knuckles touching this centre, and the hands vertical, facing each other in front of your chest.
- As you inhale, imagine breathing energy up from the base of the spine, into your spiritual heart. Exhale in a relaxed way.
- Continue breathing this way for several minutes, noticing any change in how you feel. Remember that the heart is the centre of love. Let love come back into your life.

Closing Thoughts

Bipolar disorder seems to me to be a sickness that came when I had exhausted the grace of God, or the goodwill of the universe, to put it another way. Don't think of it as "you pushed it too far this time, and now you are going to get it," but rather a case of having nothing in the bank account and overdrawing until there was no credit left. I prayed a lot to be relieved of the illness, and that must have had an effect. I advise you to keep praying as well. Doing the exercises I described will do wonders toward restoring the grace you will need if you want to get well. Reaching out a helping hand to others in need will also help you, but remember the adage "you can't give away what you don't have."

CHAPTER 10:
Advice for Those Trying to Help

This section addresses advice toward people in the bipolar sufferer's life who are wondering what they can do to help. I will address doctors, spouses, family and friends. My perspective for writing this is my experience of what helped me throughout my illness.

Doctors. Throughout my various hospitalizations, I was treated by a series of doctors. All told, I had consultations with six different doctors. Here is how I would rate them, in order, from least to most effective:

- A fearful doctor who was afraid of me and wouldn't let me go outside even for five minutes of fresh air, under supervision from the orderly, with the other patients. She also had no sense of humour. She saw to it that I wouldn't leave the hospital until I was doped up with enough drugs to overmedicate a horse (that is a small exaggeration).

- A hard-nosed, take-no-crap doctor who mercilessly informed me I would probably need drugs for the rest of my life. She didn't take time to listen to anything I said or to my family's concerns either.

- A strange doctor who played mind games with me. I am not sure where to rank him actually, because he was the one who switched my medication to two other drugs I can really tolerate well and am still taking now. All in all, I owe him a big favour for that! (I still think he is strange, though ...)

- An intellectual doctor who often took time to listen but didn't get overly involved in helping. She was more like a casual acquaintance you could talk to, but she stayed neutral.

- A helpful doctor who projected the feeling of kindness. She also took time to listen and helped decide that I should not be forced by court order to take medication on my last visit to the hospital. I am glad she decided that.

- A very caring doctor who was not afraid to come see me by herself even when I was in the pink room and not on any medication. She took the time to listen. She was not above trying to trick me into taking my medication on numerous occasions, but she had a good sense of humour. She projected a feeling of love for her patients and told me she was a spiritual person.

Looking back, I guess my own attitudes coloured how I was treated by the doctors, because they are only human too. If you are a doctor reading this, it might be appropriate to ask yourself where you would be in this range of behaviours and whether you would like to increase your effectiveness by moving up on it. Care about and be kind to the patients, and if you can, love the patients, and you may see miracles happen in their lives. You are more than a medication prescription expert, more than a provider of services. Give your patients some hope by telling them their lives are not over. Talk about the benefits of medication if they are afraid—don't emphasize side effects and set up a self-fulfilling prophecy. I am grateful for the help psychiatrists have given me through the years. I was often an obstinate patient who must have tried their patience at times.

Spouses. My wife had a very hard time with my bipolar

episodes. She saw me at my worst, and it was up to her to have me put in the hospital on three separate occasions. She also endured my depression in 2002 with great difficulty. I am a cheerful, optimistic person by nature, and this episode was probably the most difficult time in our marriage, placing considerable strain on it.

I am blessed to have had my wife stand by me throughout the episodes. She also refused to listen to insanity, which helped me snap out of it. Her love and caring and constant visits to me in the hospital were a great comfort to me. The time you can spend with your spouse while he is coming down from a manic episode will greatly help and will be a memory that will enhance your relationship. Try to forgive any bad behaviour your spouse exhibits and just love him.

When I was depressed, I was a large psychological burden to my wife. I was being a "bummer" to her. Some ill part of me was trying to bring her down with me. She refused to put up with it, as well she should have. If you are the spouse of a depressed person, realize that you can't help by drowning with him or her. Your first priority is to maintain your health and sanity. Get some space from the depressed person. Go exercise, or spend time with friends. Encourage him or her to talk to a psychologist, go to a support group, or buy a book that will help. If you can listen for a little while, you may be able to help somewhat, but don't go beyond your limits and get drained.

Family. For coping with trauma associated with bipolar disorder, it may be beneficial for parents, siblings and children to see a psychologist. Parents, out of a desire to be loyal, may resist the diagnosis of bipolar. This is not likely to be helpful. The most parents should do is to seek a second opinion for their children and be content with whatever the consensus diagnosis is. Parents may feel they know their children better than anyone, but they simply must trust the expert diagnosis of specialist psychiatrists who are in a position to objectively observe and come to conclusions, regardless of what the patient was like when he was five years old.

Brothers and sisters may be greatly shocked by whatever trauma produces a bipolar episode, as well as the episode itself. In such a case, a temporary dose of antianxiety medication may be appropriate. This is an assessment that must be made by a psychologist or psychiatrist. Brothers and sisters, especially if they have a close rapport with the bipolar individual, may be able to help in many ways. For instance, I described how my brother helped convince me to take my medication during my last hospitalization.

As far as children's needs go, it's important that children be protected in such a way that the illness will not be passed on to them. There may be genetic predisposition toward bipolar disorder in children whose parent(s) have had episodes, which only adds to the importance of sheltering the children. It is important to remember that just because we have genetic predispositions, it does not doom us to suffer any illness. Imagine the impact a parent could have if he or she were able to tell a child he or she has been healed of bipolar disorder, or that with medication, there is no reason to even think about the condition and it no longer has an effect on the parent's life.

Friends. The important thing is to let the bipolar person know that you still care about and haven't forgotten him or her. Sending cards or flowers to the home or the hospital would be a nice gesture. I was really touched when friends from work sent me some plants when I was hospitalized. Visiting is also appreciated.

Something not to overlook is that you can help by supporting the people closest to the sufferer. A phone call to the husband, wife or parents, or some food gifts would have a big impact, for example. Let them know they are not alone. This was something that my friend did for my wife while I was ill, and I haven't forgotten it.

Conclusion

Now you know my story and have heard me describe things that I have shared with few people before now. Many readers may think I am still crazy! The truth of the matter is that I can see the world from several different points of view, including the material and spiritual. The most powerful is the spiritual point of view, the province of love, where miracles abound. To get better from bipolar disorder, to be really healed, may well require you to break through into this new dimension. I have tried to give you some assistance by providing my example and by giving some tips and exercises that will help.

It's up to you now. Perhaps it's time to make a new beginning to your life and take things in a different direction. Or the more apt wording may be: to take things to a different dimension.

With love and blessings,
B. Robert Jameson

Printed in Great Britain
by Amazon.co.uk, Ltd.,
Marston Gate.